Discovering

CORINTHIANS

by Gene Sanford

EDITOR
    Alan E. Johnson

EDITORIAL ASSISTANTS
    Sherry L. Evilsizor
    Nancy Noemi Castillo

Copyright 1993 by
Beacon Hill Press of Kansas City

ISBN: 083-411-4607

Contents

Introduction

This study book has been created with the prayer that the Word of God will find a place in your heart and mind so that you will be equipped to be an effective disciple of Jesus Christ in the midst of the contemporary pagan culture you face each day.

If you are using this study book as a part of a Bible study group, then you are using it to its best benefit. In your group you will learn to trust each other as you discover 1 and 2 Corinthians and share truths that will help you learn from each other. There is a personal time of discovery to complement each group session, which will lead you into greater insights. *Discovering Corinthians* is both an excellent group workbook and a personal workbook.

If you do not have a group to study with, you can still gain great benefit from using all the studies on your own. Simply adapt the group questions when needed.

If you are using this study book as a part of a Bible quizzing program, you will be getting the full benefit out of quizzing by doing so. But be careful! The temptation to slack off on your discovery workbook when you prepare for tournaments will come at one time or another. Don't give in to that temptation! Gain the full benefit of memory work and application of biblical principles to your life as a disciple of Jesus Christ.

You are now invited to begin this special journey through 1 and 2 Corinthians with Personal Discovery No. 1. Before you begin, pause for a moment of prayer, asking God to bless the time you give to the study of His Word, and to give you the desire to grow in your relationship with Him. And be prepared to make some exciting changes in your life!

SPECIAL INSTRUCTIONS:
Each Personal Discovery is divided into five sections. All five can be done at once, but it will be more manageable—and probably more meaningful—if you do one section per day. In this way, the Personal Discoveries can be used as guides for your personal devotional times, as well as preparation for the Discovery Group sessions.

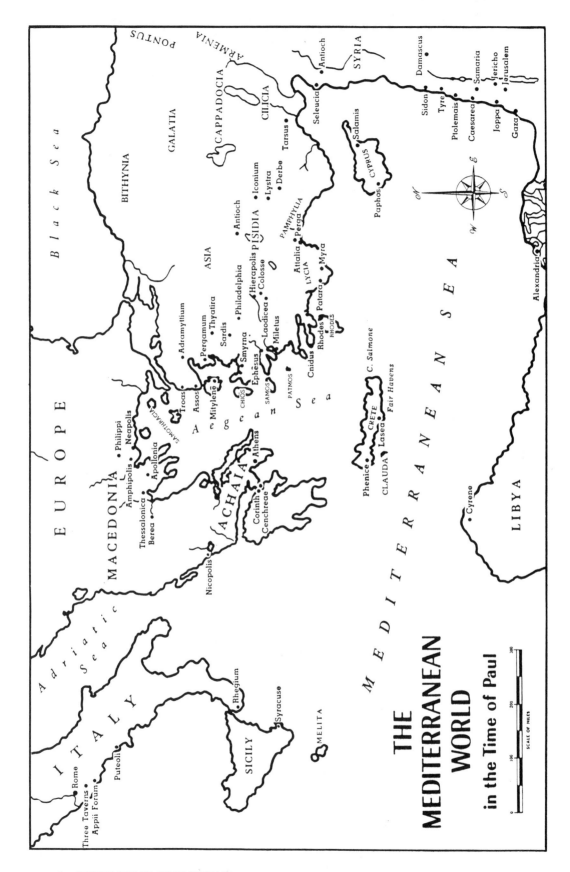

THE
MEDITERRANEAN
WORLD
in the Time of Paul

Outline of Corinthians

1 CORINTHIANS

I. Getting Along with Others (1:1-31)
   A. Relationships are important (1:1-3)
   B. Be thankful for what God gives (1:4-9)
   C. The things that divide a church (1:10-17)
   D. God's wisdom rejects division (1:18-25)
   E. Our common calling draws us together (1:26-31)

II. God's Wisdom in Christ (2:1-16)
   A. The preaching of the Cross draws us together (2:1-5)
   B. God's wisdom unites us (2:6-16)

III. Spiritual Maturity Creates Unity (3:1-23)
   A. Spiritual immaturity divides (3:1-4)
   B. Leaders who are a team unify (3:5-23)

IV. Those Who Share the Gospel (4:1-21)
   A. Faith stewards (4:1-5)
   B. Humble servants (4:6-13)
   C. Spiritual parents (4:14-21)

V. Don't Condone Immorality (5:1-13)

VI. Don't Compromise the Witness (6:1-20)
   A. Settle your own differences (6:1-11)
   B. Don't let your body lead you astray (6:12-20)

VII. Sex, Marriage, and Divorce (7:1-40)
   A. Guidelines for sexual intimacy (7:1-9)
   B. The religiously mixed marriage (7:10-16)
   C. Being content with present status (7:17-24)
   D. Creating stability in uncertain times (7:25-40)

VIII. Let Love Control Knowledge (8:1-13)

IX. The Model for Leadership (9:1-27)
   A. Laying aside rights (9:1-14)
   B. Every person's servant (9:15-23)
   C. Developing self-discipline (9:24-27)

2 CORINTHIANS

1 Foolishness and Wisdom

STUDY SCRIPTURE: 1 Corinthians 1:1—2:16

KEY VERSE: "For the message of the cross is foolishness to those who are perishing, but to us who are being saved it is the power of God" (1 Corinthians 1:18).

Personal Discovery

1. WELCOME TO 1 CORINTHIANS

When beginning a study of any portion of the Bible, one of the first questions you have to ask yourself is, "What kind of writing is this?" It's the Bible, of course. It's holy writing. It's all about how to be a Christian.

Yes, but in addition to that, what *kind* of writing is it? In many ways the Bible is an *anthology*. You've probably had to carry around one of those heavy literature books for an English class that has all kinds of poetry, short stories, drama, and essays in it. That's an anthology. The Bible is an anthology, too, because it contains many different kinds of writing. We have **history** in books like Genesis, 1 and 2 Kings, and the Book of Acts. We have **poetry** in books like Psalms and other scattered chapters in the Old and New Testaments. And, among other kinds of writing, we have **letters.**

A big chunk of the New Testament is taken up with letters, most of them written by the apostle Paul to the various congregations and people he met on his several missionary journeys. That is the kind of writing we encounter in 1 and 2 Corinthians.

Corinth was an important city in the ancient world. In fact, it was the third most important city in the Roman Empire. It was located strategically at the intersection of two important travel and trade routes, one going north and south, the other going east and west. It was a wealthy city, given to excess, and known throughout that part of the world for its vice and debauchery.

Paul visited Corinth on his second missionary journey, spending a year and a half there and founding a church, all described in Acts 18:1-18. A couple of years later he wrote the Christians in Corinth a series of letters. Although some of those letters have been lost, we have at least two of them preserved, known as 1 and 2 Corinthians.

Apparently Paul wrote the letter we call 1 Corinthians for two reasons: a group of Corinthians had visited the apostle and told him that there was trouble in the young church (see 1:11), and the church had written him a letter containing a number of questions about specific concerns (see 7:1).

Before you dig into this book chapter by chapter, it would be very helpful for you to get a broad overview of the entire letter. You can do that in less than an hour by skimming through the entire book. If your Bible has section titles, read these and then read one or two verses in each section. Don't try to read every verse (unless you have a couple of hours). Just get acquainted with this intriguing letter. Do it *right now*, before you read any further in this manual.

After you have skimmed the entire Book of 1 Corinthians, complete these statements:

▶ I think the main message of 1 Corinthians is . . .

▶ One section that really interests me is . . .

▶ One question that I'd like to have answered is . . .

▶ The most important thing that 1 Corinthians says to me personally today is . . .

2. OVERVIEW

Before we begin a detailed study, read the first two chapters of 1 Corinthians at one sitting. It will only take you a few minutes. Try to read it as eagerly as you would if you had just pulled a letter from someone very important out of the mailbox. After you have done so, answer these questions:

▶ What is your immediate reaction to the *tone* of these chapters?

▶ Is there anything in these chapters that surprises you?

▶ What in these chapters do you want to explore in more depth?

3. TROUBLE IN RIVER CITY (AND CORINTH TOO)! (1:1-17)

After his usual friendly greetings (vv. 1-9), Paul plunges right into the problems he had heard about. Because this letter was written before churches began to erect buildings, the church met in the homes of the believers. Since there were way too many Christians in Corinth to meet in one home, various smaller groups began to form and take on their own identity. Apparently some of these groups had adopted various Christian leaders as *their* leader, and rivalries between the groups soon erupted.

Read 1 Corinthians 1:1-17 and then answer these questions:

▶ If you stopped reading after verse 9, what sort of letter would you expect to follow?

▶ Your school has a team name (the Tigers, the Spartans, the Wolverines), a school song, a school mascot, and school colors, all prominently used and displayed at sporting events. In Corinth there were apparently at least four "teams" in the church. How were these "teams" identified? (Note: "Cephas" was the Greek name for the apostle Peter.)

▶ What was wrong with each of these "teams" claiming a different leader?

▶ Do you see any parallels between what was going on in Corinth and the present church?

4. WILL ALL THE "BRAINS" PLEASE STAND? (1:18—2:5)

One of the things that all Greeks were proud of was their philosophy. That was true for Corinth as well. The city was filled with men eager to expound at great length on any subject. No doubt some of this fondness for philosophy and intellectual debate entered the church.

Read 1:18—2:5 and answer these questions:

▶ At first glance, it appears that Paul is putting down education and intelligence. But we know that Paul himself was a brilliant scholar. He uses the term "foolish" to highlight one of the most important aspects of Christianity. What do you think that is?

▶ Although it is important to become as informed as possible, especially about things that really matter like the Bible and theology, it is also important not to lose sight of the simplicity of the message of Christ. Can you put that message in one simple sentence?

▶ In the early centuries of Christianity, the Church spread fastest among the lower classes, just as it has in every great national revival since. Why do you think Paul reminds the Corinthians of their lowly beginnings in verses 26-31?

▶ Paul even reminds them that when he was with them, he did not use sophisticated arguments or present himself as some great man (2:1-5). What is Paul trying to teach the Corinthians by his own example?

5. SHHH, I'VE GOT A SECRET (2:6-16)

Continuing with his line of thought, Paul further explains what he means about not being too dependent on human wisdom and intelligence. Here he introduces the idea of the Holy Spirit as the Revealer of God's truth to those who listen to Him.

Read 2:6-16 and answer these questions:

▶ Paul talks about "God's secret wisdom" in verse 7. What do you think this secret is?

▶ Paul would probably be amused at the courses in the Bible taught in high schools and colleges today that approach the text as just another literature book. What critical element of understanding spiritual things is missing from these courses?

▶ You're at the beginning of a Bible study. The manual you're holding in your hand is, we hope, written with intelligence and knowledge. You're being encouraged to study and use your mind to explore these passages. But have you taken the time to ask the Holy Spirit to help you understand what these verses are about? Why don't you do that right now. You just might learn a secret!

Discovery Group

STUDY SCRIPTURE: 1 Corinthians 1:1—2:16

KEY VERSE: 1 Corinthians 1:18

It's Bible Study Time

The teens of Westgate Church are arriving for the first session of their fall Bible study group. Let's stand at the door and watch.

There's **Sara the Scholar,** walking up the steps to the church, carrying two huge bags that appear to be quite heavy. *Hey, Sara, what's in those bags?*

I've got a Bible encyclopedia, a Bible dictionary, three different commentaries, an atlas of the Holy Land, a 12-foot time chart, Bible study guides from two different bookstores, and a super new Bible study program for my computer, which my kid brother Sam is carrying. I'm all set to tackle any problem or question that comes up tonight!

And there's **Easy Eddie,** strolling up the sidewalk with nothing but his pocket New Testament in hand. *Hey, Eddie, aren't you prepared for tonight's study?*

You bet I'm prepared. I've got the Word right here. What else do I need? I mean, all you have to do is read what's written, right? It's all there in black and white!

And here comes **Praying Paul,** tripping on the cracks in the sidewalk, since his eyes are closed. *Hey, Paul, what are you doing?*

Can't you see? I'm praying. We're going to be studying the Holy Bible tonight. You've got to wrap yourself up in prayer, or you won't understand the Scriptures. God's Word is mysterious and full of hidden messages, and only the person who is tuned in to the Holy Spirit can unravel the secrets!

What a Bible study this is going to be! These teens probably won't get past verse 1 before Sara, Eddie, and Paul are embroiled in an argument.

So who's right? Who has the right approach to studying the Bible? Which of these three is closest to how **you** came to the Bible study session today?

Human Wisdom vs. God's Power

In 1 Corinthians 1:17—2:5, Paul sets up a contrast between human wisdom and God's power. Let's look at how he does that.

1. Paul's Own Example (1:17; 2:1-5)
   a. How does Paul describe the way that he first approached the Corinthians?

   b. What was Paul's reason for this approach?

2. The Corinthians' Example (1:26-31)
   a. What kind of people were the Corinthians when Paul first encountered them?

   b. What is important about their place in the world?

3. The Example of Christ (1:18-25)
   a. What is the "message of the cross" (v. 18)?

   b. Why would that message appear so "foolish" to people of the world?

Another Kind of Wisdom

Remember Easy Eddie from the first activity? Let's hear how he responds to the passages we've just read:

> This is great stuff! Paul is saying that wisdom is bad, learning is stupid, and philosophy is useless (1:20)! See, I was right! Let's throw away all the books, forget about studying, and just kick back and relax. Who wants to be smart anyway?

Not so fast, Eddie. Paul isn't putting down *all* wisdom. He's got another kind of wisdom in mind. Let's find out what kind of wisdom the apostle *does* like by reading 1 Corinthians 2:6-16 and hunting the characteristics of the wisdom Paul is describing:

1. Verse 7:

2. Verse 8:

3. Verse 10:

4. Verse 12:

5. Verse 13:

Now summarize these verses by describing the kind of wisdom Paul is talking about in your own words:

Fools Become Wise

Look back at the three teens described in the first activity. Based on what you have learned, what would you say to each of them?

1. **Sara the Scholar:**

2. **Easy Eddie:**

3. **Praying Paul:**

Now take a few moments and look at your own approach to the Bible and to spirituality as a whole. What are you trusting in, man's wisdom or God's power?

2 Babes in Christ

STUDY SCRIPTURE: 1 Corinthians 3:1—4:21

KEY VERSE: "Brothers, I could not address you as spiritual but as worldly—mere infants in Christ. I gave you milk, not solid food, for you were not yet ready for it. Indeed, you are still not ready" (1 Corinthians 3:1-2).

Personal Discovery

1. OVERVIEW

In chapters 3 and 4, Paul continues to address the divisions in the Corinthian church. Read these chapters at one sitting, and then answer these questions:

▶ What themes did you find repeated from the first two chapters?

▶ What in these chapters caught your attention?

▶ What passage would you like to dig into further?

▶ What passage puzzled or troubled you?

2. BABIES, SEEDS, AND FOUNDATIONS (3:1-15)

Good teachers and preachers always look for just the right illustration or metaphor to help their listeners understand what they are trying to say. In these 15 verses, Paul uses three different metaphors to describe what is happening in Corinth. As you read these verses, try to picture in your mind each of these illustrations.

After reading these verses, answer these questions:

▶ When Paul founded the Corinthian church just a few years earlier, he obviously taught them the most elementary truths of Christ. What does he compare those truths to (v. 2)?

▶ How do you think the Corinthians might have responded to being called "infants"? Why does Paul say that they are *still* infants?

▶ In verse 6 Paul shifts to a different illustration, one concerning seeds. Do these verses remind you of a passage in Matthew? (See Matthew 13:1-23.) Why does Paul reject any claim of importance in the "growing" of the church at Corinth?

▶ Once again Paul shifts metaphors. In verse 10 he begins talking about a building. What does he say the foundation of a spiritual building must be? What happens if inferior materials are used in the building?

▶ As you look at *your* spiritual life, do you think you are an infant or an adult? Is the seed of the gospel thriving in your life or withering? What kinds of materials are you using to build your spiritual life?

3. GOD'S TEMPLE (3:16-23)

Keeping with the thought of building, Paul moves to an image his Jewish readers would quickly identify with: the Temple. And then he shifts back to his previous thoughts about foolishness and wisdom.

Read these verses and then answer these questions:

▶ The "you" in verse 16 is plural, meaning that Paul was thinking of the entire Corinthian church as "God's temple." What behavior among the Corinthian Christians would contribute to the destruction of this temple? What behavior among Christians today could put the temple at risk?

▶ It is obvious from Paul's continued discussion of wisdom that there were some in Corinth who had been attempting to set themselves above others as wiser and more knowledgeable. What is Paul's suggestion to them (v. 18)?

▶ After all the talk about the "teams" in Corinth (Paul's, Apollos's, Cephas's), how does Paul seek to unite these factions (v. 23)?

4. APOSTLES ON TRIAL (4:1-13)

There is nothing wrong with team spirit unless it becomes an excuse to put down the opposing team. At any sporting event you can find people who don't understand good sportsmanship and who think that booing the other team makes their team look better. Apparently in the Corinthian "teams" there was some of this behavior. And since the "teams" were taking the names of various apostles, it was the apostles themselves who were being put down.

Read how Paul responds to this situation in 4:1-13 and then answer these questions:

▶ Apparently some of the factions in Corinth had been really letting Paul have it. How does he respond to their criticism in verses 3-4?

▶ In verse 7 Paul asks, "What do you have that you did not receive?" Have you ever heard people who appeared to be bragging about their spirituality? Have you ever been tempted to be proud of your spiritual growth? What does Paul say to *you* in this verse?

▶ In verses 9-10 Paul uses irony to make his point. How do you feel about the tone of these verses? Do you think Paul is angry here? Or is he merely speaking forcefully?

▶ In verses 11-13 Paul drops the irony and speaks literally. If you read the Book of Acts, you will find the stories of apostles being shipwrecked, beaten, and persecuted. Why do you think Paul reminds the Corinthians of these events?

5. FATHER LOVE (4:14-21)

None of us enjoys being scolded by our parents. And Paul has done a pretty thorough job of scolding the Corinthians. But in this section he explains to them that the harsh words he has used were written with the love of a father.

After reading these verses, answer these questions:

▶ If Paul's purpose in writing wasn't to make the Corinthians feel ashamed (v. 14), what was his purpose?

▶ Verse 16 may sound strange to you. It almost sounds like Paul is boasting. Compare this verse with 1 Corinthians 11:1. What is Paul really saying?

▶ Timothy was one of Paul's closest associates. You can read a little about him in Acts 16:1-3. What was Timothy's mission in Corinth to be?

▶ Most of us have heard the words "Just wait until your father gets home!" Paul uses a little of that kind of warning in verses 18-21. In light of everything Paul has written to this point, if he were to visit *your* youth group, do you think he would come "with a whip, or in love and with a gentle spirit"?

Discovery Group

STUDY SCRIPTURE: 1 Corinthians 3:1—4:21

KEY VERSE: 1 Corinthians 3:1-2

You Must Have Been a Beautiful Baby!

On the chart below, list your favorite things for the ages indicated:

Your favorite:	1 Year Old	5 Years Old	12 Years Old	Now
1. Food				
2. Toy				
3. TV Show				
4. Article of Clothing				
5. Word				

But Look What's Happened Since!

Don't you just love it when someone like a teacher or a parent says, **"You're acting like a baby!"** But, admit it, sometimes it's true, isn't it?

The Corinthians were apparently having the same problem with permanent infancy in their spiritual lives.

1. **LEGITIMATE BABIES.** Read the story of Paul's visit in Corinth during his missionary journey (Acts 18:1-18) along with 1 Corinthians 1:26-27 and 3:1-2*a*. What condition were the Corinthians in when Paul first preached to them? What was their response to Paul's preaching?

2. **PROLONGED INFANCY.** In 3:2*b* Paul says that the Corinthians are *still* spiritual babies. When someone says to you, "You're acting like a baby!" they don't mean that you weigh eight pounds, or that you are still wearing diapers, or that you are nearly bald. They are talking about your *behavior.* Look at the following verses and identify the behaviors that prove that the Corinthians were still spiritual infants:

a. 1 Corinthians 1:10-12

b. 1 Corinthians 1:20

c. 1 Corinthians 3:3-4

d. 1 Corinthians 3:18-21

e. 1 Corinthians 4:6-7

f. 1 Corinthians 4:18-20

Which Would You Prefer: Strained Carrots or a Big Mac?

Paul says that when he was with the Corinthians, he gave them spiritual "milk" (3:2). Paul goes on to say that the Corinthians are still not ready for spiritual "solid food."

1. If you were to preach the gospel to people who had never heard of Jesus, what things would you have to teach them about? In other words, what was the spiritual "milk" that Paul probably had to give the Corinthians?

2. What do you think are some of the ingredients of adult spiritual food?

3. What are some of the behaviors of mature Christians?

What's on Your Menu?

On the spiritual growth scale below, place a check where you think you are right now:

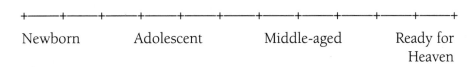

Newborn   Adolescent   Middle-aged   Ready for
                                                           Heaven

What kind of spiritual food has been on your menu lately?

☐ Infant Formula

☐ Strained Carrots and Peas

☐ Cookies and Milk

☐ Burgers and Fries

☐ Strawberry Shortcake

☐ Fresh Vegetables

☐ Steak

If you're not happy with your answers, what can you do *this week* to start growing spiritually?

3 Everybody's Doing It—or Are They?

STUDY SCRIPTURE: 1 Corinthians 5:1—7:40

KEY VERSE: "Do you not know that your body is a temple of the Holy
Spirit, who is in you, whom you have received from God? You are not
your own; you were bought at a price. Therefore honor God with
your body" (1 Corinthians 6:19-20).

Personal Discovery

1. OVERVIEW

Apparently Paul was aware of some very specific problems and questions in the Corinthian church. The next three chapters concern matters of sexual immorality, lawsuits among Christians, and marriage.

Read these three chapters at one sitting, and then answer these questions:

▶ Is there anything in these chapters that surprises you?

▶ Is there anything in these chapters that seems familiar to you?

▶ What section would you like to explore further?

▶ What questions do you want to have answered as we study these chapters?

2. ONE BAD APPLE (5:1-13)

You have probably heard the old saying that one bad apple spoils the barrel. Just because it's old doesn't mean it's not true! In the Corinthian church there was one *very* bad apple, and Paul is insisting that, for the sake of the church, that apple be removed.

After you have read these 13 verses, answer these questions:

▶ Since Paul does not use the words "incest" or "adultery" to describe the situation referred to in verse 1, it is probable that the man in question was living with his stepmother, perhaps after the death of his father. This immoral situation was one not even the pagans would accept. What does Paul instruct the Corinthian church to do about this man?

▶ Paul's language in verse 5 sounds harsh: "Hand this man over to Satan." Paul is saying, in effect, if this man wants to live a sinful life, let him do it among sinners, not in the church. But note how the verse ends: "so that . . . his spirit [may be] saved on the day of the Lord." What do you think is Paul's primary motive here, punishment or redemption?

▶ What bothered Paul as much as the man's immorality was the Corinthians' acceptance of it. Apparently they were "proud" (v.

2) and "boasting" (v. 6) that they were liberal enough to tolerate this situation in their midst. What is the problem with this man being in the church? (Hint: verse 6 is a lot like the "rotten apple spoiling the bunch" saying.)

▶ Paul indicates in verse 9 that he had written a previous letter to the Corinthians, a letter that has been lost. In that letter, he instructed the Corinthians not to associate with sexually immoral people. He makes a point of saying that he doesn't mean not to associate with sinners at all, because we all have to live in daily contact with non-Christians. The point is that such people should not be welcomed into the fellowship and membership of the church. Imagine for a moment that someone behaving openly in a sinful manner were a Sunday School teacher in your church. What kind of problems do you think that would create? How would the people *outside* the church react?

3. DON'T TAKE THE LAW INTO YOUR OWN HANDS—TAKE HIM TO COURT! (6:1-11)

Imagine tuning in to "People's Court" and seeing two members of your church board suing each other! How would that make you feel? What would the people of the community say? Well, that's exactly what was happening in Corinth.

Read these verses and then answer these questions:

▶ The first problem is that the Christians were taking their disagreements before non-Christian courts. Here Paul says an interesting thing about the Day of Judgment: "Do you not know that the saints [meaning Christians] will judge the world?" (v. 2). If, at the end of the world, Christians will help decide the fate of non-Christians, why are non-Christians being asked to decide the fate of Christians now? What is Paul's solution to this mess (v. 4)?

▶ Read Matthew 5:25 and 18:15-17. What light do these words from Jesus shed on the Corinthian problem?

► In verse 7 Paul suggests an even better solution. Compare this verse to Matthew 5:39-42. What is this better solution?

4. YOUR BODY IS A TEMPLE (6:12-20)

Once again Paul's thoughts turn toward sexual immorality and the Corinthians' apparent erroneous pride in their liberality. In this passage Paul speaks to us too.

► Paul begins this section by quoting what he has heard the Corinthians say: "Everything is permissible for me." (If you are reading in the King James Version, it is not so clear that this is a quotation. But don't misunderstand and think that Paul is saying this.) In what two ways does Paul refute this statement (v. 12)?

► Paul goes on to state that our bodies "are members of Christ himself" (v. 15). What do you think he means by this?

► In verse 16 Paul quotes Genesis 2:24, which reads, "For this reason a man will leave his father and mother and be united to his wife, and they will become one flesh." How does this truth apply to sexual immorality?

► In the Old Testament, the Jews believed that God lived in the Temple in Jerusalem. In 3:16 Paul says that the church is God's temple. Now he says that each individual Christian is also God's temple (6:19). What impact does (or should) that truth have on the idea of sexual relations?

► Paul says, "You are not your own; you were bought at a price" (vv. 19b-20a). What "price" is Paul referring to?

5. TO MARRY OR NOT TO MARRY (7:1-40)

This is a long section—an entire chapter. But it is all a response to a question the Corinthians had apparently asked in a letter to Paul. We don't have that letter, unfortunately, but we can infer that the question went something like this: "Is it better for Christians to get married or be single?"

Hold on to your hats. You might be surprised at some of Paul's answers. After you have read this chapter, answer these questions:

▶ Several times in this chapter Paul says that it is better for a Christian to be unmarried (vv. 1, 7-8, 26-28, 38). He indicates that he himself is unmarried (vv. 7-8). These verses (like all Scripture) must be understood in the context in which they were written. The 1st-century Christians expected Jesus to return at any moment. They considered themselves the "advance forces" to get the world ready for an imminent judgment. You might say that because of that context these verses don't apply to us. On the other hand, has the context really changed? Are we not, even in the 20th century, still God's advance forces? Should we not be preparing for an imminent return of Christ? What do you think?

▶ In verses 32-35 Paul explains why he thinks it is easier for Christians to be single than to be married. Do you agree with his reasoning?

▶ Even though Paul thinks singleness has more advantages than marriage, he doesn't forbid marriage. What understanding of human nature leads Paul to allow for marriage? (See verses 2, 9, 36.)

▶ It is important that we see clearly that Paul is not condemning sexual relations in this chapter. Indeed, he indicates that married couples *should* have an active and healthy sex life (vv. 3-5). What is your response to this?

▶ Paul has a lot to say about divorce here too. Read verses 10-16 and summarize Paul's instructions.

Discovery Group

STUDY SCRIPTURE: 1 Corinthians 5:1—7:40
KEY VERSE: 1 Corinthians 6:19-20

Family Living

It's third period, and the students at Central High School are finding their seats in Mrs. Johnson's "Family Living" class. Today's topic is "Teen Sex." Let's listen in as Mrs. Johnson polls her students for their opinions:

Maria: I've been taught all my life that a person should wait until they're married before they have sex. But I think that's absolutely archaic. Maybe being a virgin until marriage made sense in the 18th century, I don't know. But now it's ridiculous. *Nobody* waits until they're married. At least, nobody *I* know! Besides, it's fun.

Jason: But what about love? Don't you think it's important to be in love before you have sex? I mean, promiscuity isn't cool. But if two people really care about each other and plan to get married, then sex is OK.

Frank: I agree with Maria, but I want to add something. Sex before marriage is OK as long as you're careful to prevent pregnancy. What two people do is their business—as long as a third person isn't added. It's so easy these days to prevent an "accident" from happening. Teen sex is great; teen pregnancy isn't.

Tina: And don't forget about preventing disease. We've already talked about STDs—sexually transmitted diseases—in this class. Today it can be a matter of life and death. I agree with Maria and Frank, teen sex is OK, but you've got to play safe!

Michelle: Hold on. "Sex is OK if you watch out for this, if you watch out for that." Doesn't it make sense to anybody that those things to watch out for are precisely why sex before marriage is pretty stupid? Frank, there is no 100 percent effective way to prevent pregnancy—other than abstinence. And the same goes for disease, Tina. I mean, I'm no prude or fundamentalist or anything. I just think that the old "Just Say No" thing is still the smart thing.

Brian: Michelle's got the right answer, but she's using the wrong reasons. Sex before marriage is wrong because it's wrong. Period. The Bible says so. My church says so. God says so. If you live your life the right way, you won't even have to *worry* about things like pregnancy and disease.

1. Who do *you* agree with?

2. Who do *your friends* agree with?

3. Who do *most of the kids in your school* agree with?

Paul to the Corinthians: JUST SAY NO!

If you think 20th-century teenagers have a monopoly on sex, just read 1 Corinthians! What Paul has to say is as current as the latest episode of "The Young and the Restless."

Divide your group into five teams. Each team should explore one of these passages:

1. 1 Corinthians 5:1-5
2. 1 Corinthians 6:12-20
3. 1 Corinthians 7:1, 7-8, 26-28, 38
4. 1 Corinthians 7:2, 9, 36
5. 1 Corinthians 7:10-16

As you explore these passages, answer these questions:

a. What seems to be going on in Corinth?

b. What are Paul's instructions?

c. What are Paul's reasons for giving those instructions?

d. How do those instructions apply to us today?

Victoria's Secret

Vicky was your best friend in grade school. But during the summer after sixth grade she moved to another state. You've remained friends by exchanging letters frequently. Yesterday you got a letter from Vicky that included this paragraph:

> Remember Tim, the guy I told you about a couple of letters ago? Well, we've been dating now for three months. He is the neatest guy. He is gorgeous and he treats me really fine. I'm in love with him, and I know it's the real thing. We've talked about getting married as soon as we graduate—but that seems like such a long way off. Every time we're together, we get a little closer. Know what I mean? He's not, like, pressuring me or anything. Really, I want it as much as he does. I know my parents would have a cow if they ever found out, but I think it's just a matter of time before Tim and I go all the way. We've already talked about being "safe" if we do. I know all about that stuff. Tim's willing to do his part to make sure nothing bad happens.

OK, now it's your turn to write Vicky. What are you going to say?

Honor God

Do you not know that your body is a temple of the Holy Spirit, who is in you, whom you have received from God? You are not your own; you were bought at a price. Therefore honor God with your body.

—1 Corinthians 6:19-20

4 Making Right Choices

STUDY SCRIPTURE: 1 Corinthians 8:1—11:1

KEY VERSE: "So whether you eat or drink or whatever you do, do it all for the glory of God" (1 Corinthians 10:31).

Personal Discovery

1. OVERVIEW

The letter from the Corinthians that Paul refers to in 7:1 also contained some other concerns. In these chapters Paul answers their questions about idolatry and how to deal with the food used in pagan worship, as well as some concerns about his rights as an apostle.

Read through these three chapters at one sitting and then answer these questions:

▷ Is there anything in these chapters that confuses or concerns you?

▷ Is there anything in these chapters that stands out as something that might be helpful to you?

▷ What is the biggest question you would like to have answered about these chapters?

▷ What section of these chapters do you most want to explore in further detail?

2. WEAK CONSCIENCES AND STRONG STOMACHS (8:1-13)

What is an enterprising pagan to do with the meat left over after a sacrifice to the gods? Sell it, of course. The Corinthian market was filled with discount meat: "Only one previous owner—and he was a god!"

Read 8:1-13 and then answer these questions:

▶ The problem the Corinthians had written Paul about was this: Is it OK for a Christian to eat meat that has been used in a pagan sacrifice? Apparently there was some disagreement among the congregation about this question. Before Paul answers the question directly, he sets some ground rules. According to verses 2-3, what should be the basis for finding the answer, knowledge or love?

▶ Next Paul gives "Answer No. 1." It is a logical, knowledgeable answer and apparently the one that the "philosophers" in the Corinthian church were betting on. Summarize the answer from verses 4-6.

▶ But here comes the problem with Answer No. 1. Not everyone is smart or mature enough to realize that the idols are really nothing (v. 7). What to do about them? Laugh at their immaturity? Point out the error in their thinking? What is "Answer No. 2" (vv. 9-13)?

▶ Now, we don't have to worry too much about meat that has been offered to idols today. All we care about is the USDA seal of approval. But are there issues in our world that are similar? Can you think of a contemporary question that is like the first-century problem of meat? How would Paul's instructions help us solve that problem?

3. APOSTLES ON TRIAL, PART II (9:1-27)

Once again Paul answers the Corinthians who have been criticizing him. This time the problem seems to be about compensation. Should an apostle have to do outside work to support himself or should the congregations support him?

Read chapter 9 and then answer these questions:

▶ In verses 1-12*a* Paul argues that an apostle should not have to support himself by doing secular work while he is preaching the gospel. Can you summarize Paul's argument?

▶ In spite of this argument, Acts 18:3 tells us that Paul was a tentmaker by trade and that he supported himself in that manner during his stay in Corinth. In verses 12*b*-18, Paul explains why he did this. What was his reason?

▶ In verses 19-23 Paul reveals some of his "tactics" in preaching the gospel. What are they?

▶ The last portion of this chapter is built around an athletic illustration. Paul links the Christian life to a race. What do you think these verses mean—especially to you?

4. THOSE WHO DO NOT REMEMBER THE PAST ARE DESTINED TO REPEAT IT (10:1-13)

After stating that he hopes he "will not be disqualified for the prize" (9:27), Paul is reminded of the lessons the Israelite people learned during their exodus from Egypt. Read these verses and then answer these questions:

▶ Do you know anyone who thinks that because he is a member of a church, he is automatically going to heaven? Apparently some in Corinth had that idea. They had been baptized, they participated in the Lord's Supper, they were members of the congregation. What does Paul's reference to the Old Testament story of the Israelites in verses 1-5 say to these people?

▶ What had some of the ancient Israelites done to nullify their position as God's chosen people (vv. 6-10)? Can you think of contemporary examples of these same behaviors?

▶ Paul warns, "So, if you think you are standing firm, be careful that you don't fall!" (v. 12). But then he goes on to give a surefire preventative for falling. What is it?

▶ This whole section is one we don't want to take too lightly, nor do we want to misunderstand it. Some people read passages like this and get the idea that they are always in jeopardy of losing their salvation. These are the people who are constantly at an altar of prayer, making sure that they are still OK in God's sight. On the other hand . . . well, *you* say what the other hand is. Describe the kind of people who don't pay any attention to this kind of warning.

5. IN SUMMARY, YOU'RE FREE . . . TO DO THE RIGHT THING (10:14—11:1)

In this section Paul summarizes all that he has said in response to the Corinthians' question about eating meat that has been offered to idols. As you read this, don't let it be some archaic argument about something that has no relevance to you. Think about a contemporary ethical problem that you and your friends are dealing with, and substitute that problem in your mind for the meat-eating problem as you read.

After you have read these verses, answer these questions:

▶ Paul begins with a beautiful explanation of what happens in a Communion service (vv. 14-17). Then he draws a parallel to what happens in a pagan service (vv. 18-22). How does this answer the question about eating meat that has been sacrificed to idols?

▶ Once again Paul quotes the Corinthians as he did in 6:12, "Everything is permissible" (10:23). Then he writes a line that we should all memorize (v. 24). How does this instruction relate to the contemporary ethical problem you are thinking about?

▶ Finally in verses 25-30 Paul gives a concrete and practical answer to the Corinthians' question. Does this answer relate to your contemporary problem?

▶ In 10:31—11:1 Paul wraps up this section of the letter by rephrasing what he said in verse 24. How well do your motives stack up against these?

Discovery Group

STUDY SCRIPTURE: 1 Corinthians 8:1—11:1
KEY VERSE: 1 Corinthians 10:31

How Do You Make Ethical Decisions?

When you have to make a decision about whether an action or attitude is right or wrong, how do you usually do it?

1. ___ I just do what feels right.

2. ___ I ask my parents for advice.

3. ___ I try to find out if there is a rule or law that applies.

4. ___ I do what my friends are doing.

5. ___ I do what you see on TV.

6. ___ I figure out if anyone will be hurt by my decision.

7. ___ I do what's most advantageous to me.

What do you think are some of the most difficult ethical or moral questions you and your friends are facing?

To Eat or Not to Eat

The Christians in Corinth tried to stump Paul with this question: "Should Christians eat meat that has been offered to idols?"

Let's see how Paul decided on the right answer.

The Arguments

Pro	Con
1 Corinthians 8:4-6	1 Corinthians 8:7
1 Corinthians 8:8	1 Corinthians 8:9-10
	1 Corinthians 10:14-21

The Principles

1 Corinthians 8:1-3	1 Corinthians 10:24
1 Corinthians 8:12	1 Corinthians 10:31-32

The Decision
1 Corinthians 10:25-29

Deranged Turtles

Tom and Kathy have been invited by some of their friends to go with them to a "Deranged Turtles" concert. This is the hottest concert of the season, and everyone will be there. Tom has already accepted the invitation, but Kathy has some concerns. Let's listen in on their discussion:

TOM: Come on, Kathy. It's going to be a great concert. What's your problem?

KATHY: My problem is that I think some of the "Deranged Turtles" songs are, well, inappropriate.

TOM: Like what?

KATHY: Like the song "Who Ya Gonna Blame When the City Burns?" That is a blatantly racist song. And it promotes violence.

TOM: Give me a break, Kathy. It's just a song. No one pays attention to the lyrics.

KATHY: I bet you wouldn't say that if you were an Afro-American.

TOM: Wait a minute. How do you know so much about the song?

KATHY: I have their album.

TOM: Aha! You listen to their music! How can you turn around and say that going to the concert is wrong?

KATHY: Listening to their music in my bedroom is different from going to a public concert where everyone can see us.

TOM: How so?

Let's stop the discussion right here and give *you* a chance to participate. Using the principles that Paul used to make an ethical decision for the Corinthians, what help can you give Tom and Kathy?

How About Your Problems?

Now look back at the list of ethical and moral questions you made in the first activity. Choose one of them to discuss. How can you apply what you have learned today to this problem?

5 How the Church Should Work

STUDY SCRIPTURE: 1 Corinthians 11:2—12:31

KEY VERSE: "Now to each one the manifestation of the Spirit is given for the common good" (1 Corinthians 12:7).

Personal Discovery

1. OVERVIEW

The next problem in the Corinthian church that Paul tackles is that of disorderly worship. The apostle isn't talking about noisy teenagers or crying babies. This problem is much worse.

Read 1 Corinthians 11 and 12, and then answer these questions:

▶ What would you say is the general tone of these chapters?

▶ Is there anything in these chapters that disturbs or confuses you?

▶ What passage particularly catches your attention?

▶ What passage do you think you're going to need more help in understanding?

2. MEN AND WOMEN IN WORSHIP (11:2-16)

This is perhaps one of the most disturbing and controversial passages in the New Testament. Paul begins his attempt at helping the Corinthians bring order to their worship services. And he starts at a place that is very difficult for us in the 20th century to understand.

Read these verses and then answer these questions:

▶ What is your first reaction to these verses? Be honest!

▶ In verse 3 the word *head* means "source," not "authority." Paul is describing the order of existence:

- **God the Father is the Source of Christ the Son.**
- **Christ is the Source of man. (Paul also indicates his understanding of Christ as the active Agent in creation in 1 Corinthians 8:6 and Colossians 1:15-17.)**
- **Man is the source of woman (Genesis 2:21-22).**
  These verses must be read in conjunction with verses 11-12. Given this understanding, what is Paul saying about the relationship between men and women?

▶ Verses 4-10 and 13-16 form one of the several passages in the New Testament that *must* be understood in its historical and cultural context. The world that Paul and the Corinthians knew had very strict rules about how men and women were to dress and behave. The only women who cut their hair or went into public without a head covering were prostitutes and other women of low character. Decent and moral women wore their hair long and kept it covered in public. Why would that custom lead Paul to write what he has in these verses?

▶ How do you think a contemporary Christian is to deal with these verses? Should all women continue to wear their hair long and keep their heads covered?

▶ Can you think of modern dress customs that might also illustrate what Paul is trying to say?

3. COMMUNION CONFUSION (11:17-34)

For us Communion means a sip of grape juice and a small wafer during a Sunday worship service. In the first century, however, Communion was a part of a full meal. (Remember that Jesus initiated the ceremony while He and the apostles were eating the Passover meal.) While the "Lord's Supper" generally took on the atmosphere of an all-church potluck (Jude even calls it a "love feast" in verse 12 of his short letter), in Corinth it had become a symbol of the other problems the congregation was experiencing.

Read these verses and then answer these questions:

▶ In verses 17-22 Paul lists three behaviors that are causing the Lord's Supper to be ruined in Corinth. Can you identify those behaviors?

▶ Verses 23-26 are probably familiar to you, for they are frequently read at Communion services. Don't let their familiarity keep you from missing their meaning, however. What did Jesus mean when He said that the bread was His body and the cup His blood?

▶ Verse 26 is the key to understanding why Communion is still part of our ritual 19 centuries later. What are you doing every time you participate in this ceremony? Did you think about that the last time you took Communion?

In light of what Paul has said in verses 17-22, what do you think he means by "in an unworthy manner" in verse 27?

4. A GIFT? FOR ME? (12:1-11)

Who is more important in your church—the pastor, the Sunday School teacher, the choir member, or the custodian? If you answered with any one of those positions, you need to read these verses! Some members of the Corinthian church were convinced that they were more important than others because they had better—or at least flashier—gifts.

Read 12:1-11 and then answer these questions:

First of all, we need to distinguish between "gifts" and "talents." Many people, Christians and non-Christians alike, are born with natural talents such as a beautiful voice, athletic ability, or business insight. But "gifts" involve a special ability given by the Holy Spirit to help the church (v. 7). A person might be a fabulous singer but leave a congregation cold because there is no spirit to the song. On the other hand, a person might be a little less vocally talented and yet move a congregation to tears of joy or worship. *That* is a gift. In verses 4-6 Paul reminds the Corinthians that all gifts come from God. What does that say about their tendency to set one gift above another?

In verse 7 Paul says that "to each one the manifestation of the Spirit is given." *To each one.* That includes you as well as all the other members of your teen group! Do you believe that?

In verses 8-10 Paul lists several of the more common gifts. This list *does not* contain all the gifts that Christians might be given. Can you think of people in *your* congregation who have some of these gifts? Write their names beside the gifts they exhibit:

_____ "the message of wisdom" (or, the ability "to speak with wisdom" [Phillips])

_____ "the message of knowledge"

_____ "faith"

_____ "healing"

_____ "miraculous powers"

_____ "prophecy" (or, "speaking God's message" [TEV])

_____ "distinguishing between spirits" (or, the "ability to distinguish true spirits from false" [NEB])

We have omitted "speaking in different kinds of tongues"
and "the interpretation of tongues" from this list for now. We will
cover those gifts in the next lesson.

▶ Which gift do you think *you* have been given? One of these, or
another one?

5. THE ANKLE BONE'S CONNECTED TO THE SHIN BONE (12:12-31)

What if all the parts of your body held a contest to see which one was
the most important? What part do you think would win? What part would
lose? Would you be willing to have the losing parts removed from your
body?

That illustration is the way Paul tries in these verses to help the Corinthians understand that all members of the church are important.

Read these verses and then answer these questions:

▶ You may have heard the Church referred to as the "Body of
Christ." Here is where that idea comes from. All Christians together make up the Body of Christ. All the members of one congregation, also, form the Body of Christ. Your body has many,
many parts—but you still think of it as one unit, one body. How
is the Church like your body?

▶ In verses 14-21, Paul uses humor to get his point across. What is
his point?

▶ The Corinthians (and sometimes we as well) tended to elevate
the more important parts and ignore the less important parts.

What does Paul say we should do with less important parts in verses 22-24a? How does this relate to the parts in the Body of Christ (vv. 24b-25)?

Have you ever had a sprained ankle? Did you notice how every other part of your body seemed to work overtime to compensate for that weakness? That's what Paul is saying in verse 26. How well do you think your teen group (which is, after all, a smaller version of the Body of Christ) does at taking care of a member who is hurting?

Discovery Group

STUDY SCRIPTURE: 1 Corinthians 11:2—12:31

KEY VERSE: 1 Corinthians 12:7

Youth Group Lifeboat

Imagine that the eight members of the Eastside Church youth group are sailing to Europe when their ocean liner strikes an iceberg. All of the group members climb onto one lifeboat and are lowered into the sea. Very soon, however, they realize that the lifeboat is equipped for only six people. Either two teens must be thrown overboard, or the whole group will perish.

Listed below are the eight group members, along with a brief description. *You* must decide which two must go!

Kelly is a 17-year-old basketball star who has never professed to be a born-again Christian. He attends church irregularly, but when he comes, he usually brings several friends with him.

Bridgette is 16 years old and is known for her beautiful voice. She sings in the church choir and is frequently a featured soloist. She never misses church or Sunday School but isn't too active in the youth group.

Debbie is 14 years old and has just started attending church. She is a very shy and quiet girl and hardly ever opens her mouth. She and her mother live in a small apartment on the other side of town.

Scott, 17, is the son of a local bank president. His family contributes large amounts of money to the church, and Scott frequently pays when members of the youth group go out for pizza after church.

Steve, a high school senior, is the president of the church youth group. He has a dynamic personality and really knows how to get the group moving. He plans to be a minister.

Marianne is 18 and graduated from high school last year. Because she didn't go to college and still lives at home, she still attends the youth group meetings. She can't seem to make friends with any of the young adults at church.

Travis, 15, is the group's clown. There is no serious moment he can't break up. But there is also no one in a depressed mood he can't cheer up. The son of alcoholic parents, he is the only one in his family who attends church. He gives a clear and persuasive testimony about how God saved him during Vacation Bible School 4 years ago.

Janet, a 17-year-old, is frequently referred to as the group's "black sheep." Although she is regular in her attendance, all the kids at school know that she parties frequently with a rough crowd. She has never professed to be a Christian.

The Body of Christ

1. Have you ever heard the church referred to as the "Body of Christ"? That term comes from 1 Corinthians 12:12-27. Read those verses and pick out three or four main ideas:

2. Think for a moment of your youth group as a smaller version of the Body of Christ. (It is, you know.) Rewrite each of the following verses in your own words so that they apply to your youth group:

   a. 1 Corinthians 12:18

   b. 1 Corinthians 12:22-23

   c. 1 Corinthians 12:25

   d. 1 Corinthians 12:26

3. One of the ways the Body of Christ functions is through the individual gifts of each member. In 12:7-10, Paul lists a number of gifts that various members of a congregation might possess. The exact definition of these or other gifts is not as important as the principles *about* these gifts that Paul gives us. Again thinking of your youth group, rewrite these verses in your own words so that they apply to your group:

   a. 1 Corinthians 12:4-6

b. 1 Corinthians 12:7

c. 1 Corinthians 12:11

4. Notice that in verses 7 and 11 Paul says the same thing: gifts are given "to each one." What does that mean for your group?

Time for Your Body to Have a Checkup

Look around the room you are sitting in. Look at each member of your group. Think also about the regular members of your group who may be absent. Paul says that *each one* has a gift.

1. List the members of your group below, including yourself. By each person's name identify the gift you think that person has, including yourself.

2. Do you think each person is using his or her gift "for the common good" (v. 7) of your group? Is each person being *allowed* and *encouraged* to use his or her gift? If not, why not? Are *you* using your gift for the good of the group?

When One Cries, We All Cry

"Those parts of the body that seem to be weaker are indispensable, and the parts that we think are less honorable we treat with special honor" (1 Corinthians 12:22-23).

"If one part suffers, every part suffers with it; if one part is honored, every part rejoices with it" (1 Corinthians 12:26).

6 The Greatest of These

STUDY SCRIPTURE: 13:1—14:40

KEY VERSE: "And now these three remain: faith, hope and love. But the greatest of these is love" (1 Corinthians 13:13).

Personal Discovery

1. OVERVIEW

In chapters 13 and 14 Paul continues his discussion of the behaviors in the Corinthian church that are causing division and disruption. In the 13th chapter, however, perhaps one of the best-known chapters in the Bible, he deals with the problems by urging the Corinthians to strive for a goal of excellence.

Read chapters 13 and 14 and then answer these questions:

▶ Does anything in these chapters jump out as being something written just for you?

▶ Does anything in these chapters cause you concern or worry?

▶ How do you *feel* after you read these chapters?

▶ What section of these chapters do you know you need help understanding?

2. THE MOST EXCELLENT WAY (13:1-7)

Paul ended his discussion of the many parts of the Body and the many gifts given by the Holy Spirit in the last chapter with these words: "But eagerly desire the greater gifts. And now I will show you the most excellent way" (12:31). If that doesn't propel you into the next chapter, nothing will. Hang on for some of the finest writing in the New Testament!

Read 13:1-7 and then answer these questions:

▶ The pattern Paul set up in verses 1-3 draws our attention immediately to the subject of the chapter. The pattern goes like this: "If I exercise *[a certain gift]* but don't have *[a certain quality]*, the gift isn't worth anything." Can you identify the gifts Paul lists and the quality he says is necessary to make the gifts really worthwhile?

▶ Verses 4-7 are just packed with things to think about. Paul gives us 15 attributes or qualities of love. (The King James Version says "charity," which means love.) Make a list of each of these attributes below:

a.

b.

c.

d.

e.

f.

g.

h.

i.

j.

k.

l.

m.

n.

o.

▶ Now go back over the list you have just made. First make sure you understand what each quality on the list means. Then give yourself a score from 1 to 10 for each, with 10 meaning that this quality is *always* evident in your life, and 1 meaning that this quality is *never* evident in your life.

3. THE GREATEST GIFT (13:8-13)

Paul began this chapter by listing a few gifts or acts of service and indicating that they are nothing without love. Now he returns to the idea of gifts.

Read these verses and then answer these questions:

▶ Remember that the Corinthians were pretty "puffed up" about their gifts. What does Paul say about at least three of their gifts, compared with love, in verse 8?

▶ What is the problem with knowledge and prophecy (vv. 9 and 12)?

▶ What do you think Paul is saying to the Corinthians in verse 11?

▶ Paul says that three qualities are permanent: "faith, hope and love" (v. 13). Can you give your own definition of these three and then say why "the greatest of these is love"?

4. THE GIFT OF TONGUES (14:1-25)

If you go to an old-fashioned carnival, the booths that seem always to attract the most attention are the ones that promise a glimpse of a freak: a person who is half man and half woman; an animal with one eye in the middle of its forehead; a cat with horns. The strange and unusual always draw attention. At Corinth, some of the members were exercising a "gift" that was likewise strange and unusual: the gift of speaking in tongues.

Read these verses to see what Paul has to say about this gift, and then answer these questions:

▶ In the Book of Acts we read that on the Day of Pentecost the apostles were "filled with the Holy Spirit and began to speak in other tongues" (2:4). The context of this verse makes it clear that the apostles were speaking known languages, since each of the visitors to Jerusalem from "every nation under heaven . . . heard them speaking in his own language" (vv. 5-6). The "gift" that the Corinthians were exercising, however, was different. What is the difference? (See verses 2, 9, 16, 19, 23.)

▶ Paul does not condemn this gift, although he makes it plain that he is not very much in favor of it. Go back and read 1 Corinthians 9:20-23. Do you think this sheds some light on why Paul did not outright condemn the Corinthians' practice?

▶ Although we frequently think of **"prophecy"** as telling the future, that is not what the word really means. The gift of prophecy is what we would call the **gift of preaching.** It is the ability to proclaim God's Word in such a way that listeners understand it and are moved by it. Why is this gift so superior to the gift of tongues? (See verses 1, 3-5, 12, 24.)

> The interesting thing about the gift of tongues is that some of the speakers themselves don't understand what they are saying (see verses 14-15). How worthwhile is a gift like this, even to the one who has it?

5. TAKE YOUR TURN (14:26-40)

When you read this passage, you get the idea that the worship services at Corinth must have been more like a three-ring circus than like our fairly formal and orderly church services. That's what Paul has been getting at for four chapters.

Read 14:26-40 and then answer these questions:

> Apparently in Corinth everyone came to the worship services eager to have a part (v. 26). That much is good. But there was apparently no order or organization to their contributions. How does Paul try to remedy this situation in verses 29-33?

> Again Paul does not forbid the Corinthians to speak in tongues, but he limits the exercise of this gift in verses 27-28. What do you think is his purpose?

> Most of the early Christian churches were structured like Jewish synagogues. Even today in orthodox Jewish synagogues, the men sit on one side of the church, and the women sit on the other. The men participate in the service, but the women remain silent. This is another of those historical and cultural contexts that we must take into account in order to understand what Paul is saying in verses 34-35. We should also remember that in the time Paul was writing, women were rarely educated. In the Jewish schools, only the boys were allowed to study the Scripture. That is why the women were not allowed to participate. They could not even read the Scriptures, let alone intelligently speak about them. Even in the secular world, women's lack of education and opportunity kept them from participating in business or government. If we look at these verses in the light of what Paul wrote in 11:5-6, we get the idea that there were some women in Corinth

who were violating all local customs in their zeal to be heard, even though they lacked the training to properly comment on the Scriptures. (Would you want someone—man or woman—preaching in *your* church's pulpit who has absolutely no education and is merely saying what he or she *thinks?*) In what ways is our culture completely different from the one in which Paul wrote?

Discovery Group

STUDY SCRIPTURE: 1 Corinthians 13:1—14:40
KEY VERSE: 1 Corinthians 13:13

The Night of Patty's Revenge

It was a night that no one in the Elm Street Church youth group will forget. The teens had gathered peacefully enough for their weekly Bible study meeting, completely unaware that something strange was about to happen. Just as the meeting got under way, Patty burst into the room. (Later, witnesses would say that there was a strange look in her eye from the very beginning.)

In the previous week Patty had been reading about spiritual gifts. When she came across the gift of "discernment," she knew she was on to something. Discernment is the ability to distinguish the truth from lie. It is having such insight into another person's life that falseness stands out clearly. "That's my gift!" Patty had shouted, frightening her dog, Pookie. "I can always tell when those kids are putting on a false front. And at the next Bible study I am going to exercise my gift!"

And that's what she did. As soon as Brad, the youth group president, stood up to introduce the passage that the teens were going to study, Patty stood up too.

"Just wait a minute, Mr. Holy-on-Sundays." Oblivious to the gasps in the room, she continued. "You get up here every week like some kind of boy preacher, filled with goodness and sanctity. But I can see right through you. I know that your heart is filled with desire and lust. I know where your mind is when you're on a date with Little Miss Saintly."

Before anyone could stop her, Patty turned to Brad's girlfriend, Laura. "And you! You want us all to think that your greatest dream is to be a preacher's wife. What kind of congregation is going to put up with your addiction to soap operas and steamy novels, huh?"

Without dropping a beat, Patty grabbed another youth group member, Tony, by the back of his collar and pulled him to standing. "Don't snicker, Mr. Piety. I know how you make a show of putting your tithe in the offering plate in front of the whole congregation. But you don't really put in 10 percent, do you? That little envelope only contains a couple of dollars, when you are earning $100 a week flipping burgers at McDonald's."

By that time, several teens were making a dash for the back door. "Hold on there, Spiritual Sammy!" Patty screeched. "It's no wonder you're trying to run. You know I know about last Friday night. Five guys and five girls camping out together all night. And you promised your parents the girls were going to sleep in a separate tent. Shame on you!"

Eventually Pastor Dave, the Elm Street Church youth minister, and his wife, Evelyn, were able to wrestle Patty to the ground while someone dialed 911. Soon the paramedics whisked Patty away, never to be heard from again. That night will always be remembered as "The Night of Patty's Revenge."

The Most Excellent Way

1. Let's assume for a moment that Patty did have a genuine gift, the gift of discernment. What was wrong with the way she exercised it?

2. In 1 Corinthians 13:1-3, Paul lists three gifts and two actions that appear to be quite admirable. But something is missing. Following these three verses, fill out this chart:

Verse	Gift or Action	What's Missing	Result
1			
2			
2			
3			
3			

3. Now skip to verses 8-12, where Paul contrasts the quality of love with three of the most important gifts. What does love have that these three gifts do not?

4. In verse 13, Paul lists three eternal qualities. List those qualities here and define each one in your own words:

5. Now circle the one that Paul says is the greatest.

Love Is . . .

In 1 Corinthians 13:4-7, Paul gives 15 characteristics of love. List those characteristics in the spaces below, and then create a situation for each in which a Christian teen has the opportunity to exhibit that characteristic.

Characteristic   *Situation*

1.

2.

3.

4.

5.

6.

7.

8.

9.

10.

11.

12.

13.

14.

15.

Self-inventory Time

1. Listed below are the 15 characteristics of love. Each one is followed by a scale. Rate yourself on each of these characteristics from 1 to 5, with 1 being "I *never* exhibit this characteristic of love," and 5 being "I *always* exhibit this characteristic of love."

		Never				*Always*
a.	Love is patient.	1	2	3	4	5
b.	Love is kind.	1	2	3	4	5
c.	Love does not envy.	1	2	3	4	5
d.	Love does not boast.	1	2	3	4	5
e.	Love is not proud.	1	2	3	4	5
f.	Love is not rude.	1	2	3	4	5
g.	Love is not self-seeking.	1	2	3	4	5
h.	Love is not easily angered.	1	2	3	4	5
i.	Love keeps no record of wrongs.	1	2	3	4	5
j.	Love does not delight in evil.	1	2	3	4	5
k.	Love rejoices with the truth.	1	2	3	4	5
l.	Love always protects.	1	2	3	4	5
m.	Love always trusts.	1	2	3	4	5
n.	Love always hopes.	1	2	3	4	5
o.	Love always perseveres.	1	2	3	4	5

2. Now look back over the list and choose *one* characteristic you would like to work on. Think of one specific thing you can do to exhibit that characteristic of love *this week:*

7 Victory over Death

STUDY SCRIPTURE: 1 Corinthians 15:1—16:24

KEY VERSE: "For as in Adam all die, so in Christ all will be made alive" (1 Corinthians 15:22).

Personal Discovery

1. OVERVIEW

All too quickly we come to the end of 1 Corinthians. It has been a unique book, a difficult book, a wonderful book. Before we finish, however, there are still some ideas to consider.

Read these last two chapters at one sitting, and then answer these questions:

▶ Is there a verse or two in these chapters that seems written especially for you?

▶ Is there a verse or two you would rather Paul had not written at all?

▶ What portion of these chapters do you think you will need the most help understanding?

▶ What portion of these chapters are you the most excited about studying?

2. THE CORE OF THE GOSPEL (15:1-11)

We must never forget that 1 Corinthians was written very early in the history of the Christian Church, sometime around A.D. 55. In fact, this letter was written *before* the Gospels of Matthew, Mark, Luke, and John. The Corinthians had no New Testament in which to find the stories about Jesus that are so familiar to us. All that they knew about Jesus was what they had learned from Paul and the other missionaries.

That must have been an exciting time in which to live. But it was probably also a confusing time. What if two different visitors told two different stories about how Jesus died? Which story would you believe? And if someone in your church decided to believe something entirely different yet, to what source would you appeal to prove him wrong?

Read verses 1-11 and then answer these questions:

▶ If you were bringing the gospel to people who had never heard of Jesus, what would you tell them? What do you think are the two or three most important facts about the life and ministry of Jesus?

▶ In verse 3 Paul makes it very clear that he did not invent the message he had preached to the Corinthians. Where did he get the gospel?

▶ Verses 3-4 give us a three-point theological statement that is at the very heart of the gospel. Even though the language may be

familiar to you, don't skip over these verses. Read them slowly two or three times. What do these verses mean to you?

▶ The appearance of the risen Christ to Peter is described in Luke 24:34. The appearance to the Twelve is described in Luke 24:36-49 (and in Matthew 28:16-20; John 20:19-23, 26-29; see also Acts 1:3). The appearance to 500 disciples and to James are not recorded in the New Testament. Go back and read about these Resurrection appearances in the passages listed. What impact do you think these appearances had on the people who witnessed them? What impact did they have on the Church?

▶ You can read about Jesus' resurrection appearance to Paul in Acts 9:1-19. What is different about this appearance? Why does Paul include it in this list?

3. EAT, DRINK, AND BE MERRY, FOR TOMORROW . . . (15:12-34)

Now Paul reveals why he has addressed this important theological issue. Just like all the other issues he has written about in 1 Corinthians, this one also came from the Corinthians themselves. Apparently some of them had been doubting whether the Resurrection was a reality—for Jesus or for anyone.

Read Paul's answer to these people, and then answer these questions:
▶ The question humankind has been asking since the beginning is this: "What happens when we die?" Many, of course, answer, "Nothing. We die and that's all." But Christian theology holds that there is life after death, that death is not the end of existence. Paul says to the Corinthians that if there were no resurrection, there would be several results. Can you find three results of this in verses 13-15?

▶ What happens to our faith as Christians if the resurrection of Christ is not true (see vv. 14, 17, 19)?

▶ Genesis tells us that death came to humankind because of Adam's sin. That is what Paul is referring to in verse 22. What came to humankind because of Jesus?

▶ In verses 24-26, Paul says that death is the "last enemy" that Christ will destroy. What do you think Paul means?

▶ In verses 24-28 Paul links the resurrection with the end of time. One of the final events of this universe will be the resurrection of all those who have died. What kind of feeling does that idea give you?

▶ In verse 32 Paul quotes a line from a Greek play that we are still quoting: "Let us eat and drink, for tomorrow we die." Do you know anyone with this philosophy of life? What is wrong with this philosophy?

4. VICTORY OVER DEATH (15:35-58)

Let's be clear. Paul is talking about a bodily resurrection for all of us. He is not talking about invisible spirits floating through the air in a metaphysical soup. He is talking about a bodily form that will continue to express our personalities.

If that sounds freaky to you, it did to some of the Corinthians too. "How are the dead raised? With what kind of body will they come?" they asked (v. 35).

Read verses 35-58 for Paul's response, and then answer these questions:

▶ Paul makes it very clear that he is not talking about a reconstruction of the physical body that we have here on earth. But he has trouble explaining just what kind of body he does mean. So he resorts to metaphors, or illustrations. The first one, in verses 36-38, concerns a seed. For the next illustration, verse 39, Paul uses the animal kingdom. Paul finally refers to astronomy for a third illustration (vv. 40-41). Thinking about these three metaphors, how would you explain the kind of body Paul is talking about?

▶ Paul next resorts to a series of contrasts in verses 42-44 to explain the difference between the physical body we have now and the spiritual body we will have at the resurrection. Think about a few of the adjectives (descriptive words) Paul uses in these verses. Which kind of body sounds better to you?

▶ Finally Paul uses the same contrast he used in verse 22, the difference between Adam and Christ (vv. 45-49). In your own words, how are Adam and Christ alike? How are they different?

▶ What happens to those who are still alive at the last moment (vv. 51-53)?

▶ In verses 54-57 Paul almost begins to shout in his excitement about the things he is discussing. Do these things make **you** excited? Why or why not?

5. LAST THOUGHTS (16:1-24)

Finally the time has come for Paul to sign off. There are only a few "housecleaning" chores remaining. Read through this chapter, and then answer these questions:

▶ The first four verses of this chapter concern an offering Paul was collecting for the other churches. Paul gives some very practical advice in verse 2. How do we continue to observe that advice in our churches?

▶ In this letter Paul has said some pretty stern things to the church at Corinth. He has indicated that some members of that church have been pretty harsh in their criticism of him. What is the tone of verses 5-20?

▶ It was common for Paul to dictate his letters to a scribe, or secretary. The last four verses, however, Paul writes with his own hand. What messages does he convey in this manner?

▶ We have now reached the end of our study of 1 Corinthians. Take a few extra moments to reflect back on what we've studied. Flip through the pages of your Bible, noting section headings and any verses you might have marked. Look over the thoughts you have recorded in this manual. Have you learned, have you grown, has your spiritual life been enriched because of this study? Write a one- or two-sentence greeting to Paul as you finish this study.

Discovery Group

STUDY SCRIPTURE: 1 Corinthians 15:1—16:24

KEY VERSE: 1 Corinthians 15:22

Sad Times at Jefferson High

The members of the youth group were gathered at their usual table in the cafeteria. Unlike their normal atmosphere of hilarity, however, a dark cloud hung over their table. The same was true of most of the tables and groups in the large room.

It had been announced that morning that Kevin, one of the most popular boys at school, had been killed in an auto accident the night before. Almost everyone at Jefferson High School knew Kevin. He had been an athlete, an above-average student, a member of the school band, and president of the senior class. And now he was dead.

Since the announcement, nearly every teacher had ignored the day's lesson plans and had instead allowed the students to talk about Kevin and about their feelings. Of course everyone was grieving in his or her own way. Death had become a reality in the halls, something that teenagers don't like to think about.

Many discussions turned to the question of what happens when someone dies. One student said, "When we die, we die. That's it. 'Just like Rover, dead all over.'" Another expressed her belief in the Buddhist teaching of reincarnation, the idea that our souls continue on in another life. Many of the Christian students, of course, spoke of their belief in heaven, while others scoffed at that "old-fashioned concept."

Some students voiced their own fears about death. The death of a classmate brought it too close to home. "It's the one great unknown," one teacher had commented. The anthropology teacher talked about how every culture has created its own mythology of death and what happens after.

Mythology. Tricia, the secretary of the church youth group, rolled the word around in her head. "Is that all our belief in eternal life is—mythology?"

The ABCs of the Gospel

1. *Lesson One: Christ Was Raised from the Dead*

We like Christmas and the Babe in the manger. We like the stories of the miracles. We like the Sermon on the Mount. But none of these really distinguish Christianity from the other world religions. There is, however, one fact that does: the resurrection of Christ.

Read 1 Corinthians 15:1-8 to hear what Paul has to say about Christ's resurrection. Summarize his writing here:

2. *Lesson Two: We, Too, Will Be Raised from the Dead*

Christ's resurrection is an event without precedent. But at the end of the world, we will all experience such an event. Read 15:12-28 and summarize what Paul is saying:

3. *Lesson Three: We Will Have New Bodies*

Just as Christ had a real body after the Resurrection, we will also have bodies. But what kind of bodies will they be? Read 15:35-53 and summarize Paul's answer to this question:

4. *Lesson Four: Death, the Last Enemy, Will Be Conquered*

Throughout centuries writers of stories, composers of music, and creators of art have pictured death as an enemy. Is that an accurate picture for Christians? Read 15:54-57 and summarize what Paul says:

So What Does Death Mean to You?

In the story that opened this lesson, it was not revealed whether Kevin, the young man who had died, was a Christian. Let's suppose that he was. And let's suppose that he was a member of your youth group.

Now let's also suppose that Kevin was in several of your classes at school. Two days after Kevin's death, one of your teachers invites you to speak to the class about what Christians feel about death. What would you say?

Who's That Knocking on My Door?

If the only people who die were old people who have lived a full life, maybe it would be easier to understand. But babies die, teenagers die, young adults die. All of us die eventually.

We've all heard the saying, "Eat, drink, and be merry, for tomorrow you die." If death is simply the end, then that saying makes sense. But if there's something else after death, maybe there's also another way to approach life.

Take a few moments to think about your own death. This doesn't need to be sad, morbid, or creepy. Death is, after all, a fact of life. But think about death as a Christian. How should the ideas you have studied in this lesson affect the way you live? How would you *like* it to affect the way you live?

8 The God Who Says "Yes"

STUDY SCRIPTURE: 2 Corinthians 1:1—3:6

KEY VERSE: "For the Son of God, Jesus Christ, who was preached among you by me and Silas and Timothy, was not 'Yes' and 'No,' but in him it has always been 'Yes.' For no matter how many promises God has made, they are 'Yes' in Christ" (2 Corinthians 1:19-20*a*).

Personal Discovery

1. OVERVIEW

Welcome to 2 Corinthians (everyone loves sequels)! Some time has passed since Paul's first letter to Corinth. There has probably even been a visit to Corinth. Some old problems have been solved, some new problems have occurred.

Before we plunge into the chapter-by-chapter study of 2 Corinthians, it would be very helpful for you to get an overview of the entire letter. This book is only 13 chapters long, so you can read through it lightly in less than an hour. If the Bible you're reading from has section headings, note those and read a few verses in each section. Don't worry about reading every word or even every verse.

After you have skimmed the entire book, answer these questions:

▶ What would you say is the tone or mood of this letter?

▶ How does this letter compare with 1 Corinthians?

▶ What sections of this letter do you think you're going to need help understanding?

> Are there any verses or sections that already make you anxious to read more?

2. THE GOD OF ALL COMFORT (1:1-11)

We must remember that Paul is not writing this letter from a comfortable Barkolounger somewhere in Antioch. He is still traveling, still bringing the gospel to new converts, still facing danger and persecution. In many ways, this is a letter from the front lines, being written by a foot soldier who is experiencing quite a bit of action.

Read these opening verses and then answer these questions:

> Skip ahead just a little bit to 2 Corinthians 11:23-28. These verses give us a clue to the kind of action Paul was seeing on his missionary trips. Now look at 1:3-4. What do these verses reveal to us about the character and faith of the apostle?

> Many people erroneously think that suffering comes as the result of doing something wrong. But Paul has done nothing wrong— and yet he is suffering. How does he interpret the origin of his suffering (v. 5)?

> In verse 9 Paul gives us an insight into how trouble can actually help us. What is that insight?

3. A CHANGE OF PLANS (1:12—2:4)

In this section Paul gives us a rather sketchy view of some of the things that have happened since writing 1 Corinthians. The apostle's relationship with this congregation is very complicated. One gets the idea that the ongoing "negotiations" between Paul and the Corinthians have been difficult.

Read these verses and then answer these questions:

> It appears that Paul once again has been forced into a defensive

position by a group of Corinthians bent on criticizing him. Paul had promised the Corinthians that he would visit them twice, both on his way to Macedonia, and on his way back (vv. 15-16). But things didn't turn out that way. He wound up making only one visit—and that one was "painful" (2:1). What does Paul say in defense of his change of plans (1:12, 17, 23)?

▶ What do you think Paul means when he says that in Jesus Christ "it has always been 'Yes'" (v. 19)?

▶ Paul says that all of God's promises are ways of saying "yes" to us (v. 20). What does that mean to you?

▶ In 2:3-4 we find a reference to a previous letter, probably 1 Corinthians. What does this reference remind you of from our study of that letter?

What does your God look like?

4. A TIME TO FORGIVE (2:5-11)

Do you remember the incident about the Corinthian church member who was living with his stepmother? Read 1 Corinthians 5:1-5 to refresh your memory.

Chapter 2:5-11 probably refers to that incident. After you have read these verses, answer these questions:

> ▶ In verse 5 Paul makes it clear that the individual's sin didn't hurt the apostle as much as it did the entire congregation. Why do you think this distinction is important?

> ▶ Verse 6 indicates that the congregation did indeed punish the man. What was the punishment Paul had recommended in 1 Corinthians?

> ▶ Now that the man had been punished, what was Paul's instruction (vv. 7-8)?

> ▶ If Paul's dealing with this man is similar to how God deals with us when we sin, which would be the better term to describe God's discipline, *redemptive* or *punitive*? (Look those words up if you don't understand them.) Why?

5. WHAT IS THAT SMELL? (2:12—3:6)

As Paul traveled around the Roman Empire, he was keenly aware of his position as ambassador for Christ. And he tried to help his converts understand that they, too, shared that position.

Read these verses and then answer these questions:

> ▶ In verse 14 Paul says that "through us [God] spreads everywhere the fragrance of the knowledge of him." Then he goes on to say that to those who do not accept Christ, the aroma is "the smell of

death"; while to those receiving the gospel, it is "the fragrance of life" (vv. 15-16). What do you think you smell like to your friends?

▶ It was common in Paul's day (as it is in ours) for ambassadors and other traveling professionals to carry letters with them from former associates recommending them to new clients. Paul says in verses 2-3 that he doesn't need such a letter. Why not?

▶ If your life is a letter, "written not with ink but with the Spirit of the living God" (v. 3), what is written on it?

▶ In verse 6 Paul again uses the word "letter," but this is an entirely different subject than the one just discussed about letters of recommendation. Here he is talking about the "letter of the law." That is a phrase we still use. Someone who follows the "letter of the law" pays close attention to every technical detail of the law, even if doing so violates the "spirit of the law." Paul says that he is a minister of a "new covenant," one that operates on the principles of the "Spirit" rather than the "letter." What do you think he means?

Discovery Group

STUDY SCRIPTURE: 2 Corinthians 1:1—3:6

KEY VERSE: 2 Corinthians 1:19-20*a*

Tell Us About Your God

Ted and Celia Franklin are a young couple in their early 30s who have just moved into the neighborhood of the church. Since Pastor Williams makes a habit of calling on all the new neighbors, he stops by their house one evening. After a few moments of conversation, Ted and Celia reveal that they are not in the habit of attending church. In fact, they have some pretty strong negative feelings about church and about God. Each of them grew up in a church family but left the church in their 20s.

Let's listen in as they explain their feelings to Pastor Williams:

TED: I grew up being afraid of God. All my life I was taught that God watched me like some old-maid-school teacher, just waiting to catch me having some impure thought or indulging in something pleasurable. The rules of my church all dealt with what I *couldn't* do. It seemed that there was nothing I *could* do that was fun. I heard a lot of sermons about God being a judge who would hold me accountable for every little mistake. The threat of hell was invoked every time I misbehaved. When I was a teenager, I lived in constant panic that God would read my thoughts and discover that I was just as "sinful" as everyone else. I can relate to people who had abusive parents. I had an abusive God. Finally, I just got tired of living under such guilt and worry—so I left the church.

CELIA: I have a lot of those same kind of memories. But the God I grew up with could also be kind and loving—when He wanted to be. We were always thanking Him for His blessings, which I guess meant a warm home and food on the table. And any time someone narrowly missed being killed in some accident, we thanked God for saving their lives. But it seemed that you could never tell when God was happy or when He was angry. So I grew up doing everything I knew how in order to stay on His good side. I went to church, put money in the offering plate, read my Bible, and tried to be kind to other people. But it was like I was constantly giving treats to a monster so that he would love me and not hurt me. I decided that a God who needed so much attention wasn't worth my time.

The God of the Bible

Let's try to find out what kind of God the apostle Paul worked for. Read the passages listed below from 2 Corinthians and record what you find out about Paul, about the Corinthians, and especially about God.

1. What does this passage say about:

                      Paul   *The Corinthians*   *God*

    a. 1:3-11

    b. 1:18-20

    c. 1:21-22

    d. 2:5-10

2. Now look up the passages listed below, and note what they tell us about God:

    a. Romans 5:6-8

    b. Romans 8:28, 32

    c. 1 John 3:1, 16

Can you put what all these passages are saying about God into one or two sentences?

Test Time

Now let's take a little quiz about God. Choose the best answer in each question below:

1. What does God think about us humans?
   a. He thinks we are worms—a bunch of lying, miserable, unworthy sinners.
   b. He thinks of us as pets—creatures to be petted, played with, and trained.
   c. He thinks we are His children—to be loved, protected, and occasionally disciplined

2. What is God's basic attitude toward us?
   a. Love
   b. Anger
   c. Irritation
   d. Apathy

3. Who is God most like?
   a. Santa Claus
   b. Ebenezer Scrooge
   c. Dr. Cliff Huxtable
   d. Judge Wapner

4. What does God want for you?
   a. He wants me to be perfect.
   b. He wants me to be happy.
   c. He wants me to behave.
   d. He wants me to get what I deserve.

5. When you do something wrong, what does God do?
   a. He says, "Oh, that's OK."
   b. He gets angry and punishes me.
   c. He allows me to experience the natural consequences of my error.
   d. He loves and forgives me.

God Is on Your Side

For the Son of God, Jesus Christ . . . was not "Yes" and "No," but in him it has always been "Yes." For no matter how many promises God has made, they are "Yes" in Christ.

—2 Corinthians 1:19-20a

9 The God of Reconciliation

STUDY SCRIPTURE: 2 Corinthians 3:7—6:2

KEY VERSE: "God was reconciling the world to himself in Christ, not counting men's sins against them. And he has committed to us the message of reconciliation" (2 Corinthians 5:19).

Personal Discovery

1. OVERVIEW

In this section Paul leaves the specific problems of the Corinthian church and writes some fabulous material for us to deal with.

Read through this passage at one sitting, and then answer these questions:

▶ What portion of this passage do you think is going to be your favorite?

▶ What portion do you think is going to be your least favorite?

▶ What question do you want to have answered as we study this material more closely?

▶ What would be your prayer before we begin digging into this passage?

2. THE OLD VS. THE NEW (3:7-18)

In the last verse of our last lesson, Paul referred to the "new covenant," one that would not operate under the death-giving structure of the "letter" of the law but under the life-giving structure of the Spirit (3:6). Now he goes on to explain what he is talking about.

Read 3:7-18 and then answer these questions:

▶ The "letters on stone" (v. 7) that Paul talks about are the original Ten Commandments that Moses brought down from the mountain to give to the Israelite people. Read Exodus 24:15-18 and 34:29-35 to get the Old Testament background for this passage.

▶ Paul refers to the Old Testament system of laws, regulations, sacrifices, and rituals as "the ministry that brought death" (v. 7) and "the ministry that condemns men" (v. 9). What about the Old Testament system causes Paul to be so harsh on it?

▶ Paul uses the Old Testament story of Moses wearing a veil to cover his face in order to illustrate some contemporary things. When he says that when the Old Testament is read the Jewish people still wear a veil, he is not talking about a literal veil. What is he talking about?

▶ How does the veil of Old Testament thinking get taken off (v. 14)?

3. GOD'S GLORY IN HUMAN VESSELS (4:1-18)

Paul ended the last section with some pretty uplifting words: "And we, who with unveiled faces all reflect the Lord's glory, are being transformed into his likeness with ever-increasing glory, which comes from the Lord, who is the Spirit" (3:18). But now he's afraid that that language sounded too much like bragging.

Read chapter 4 and then answer these questions:

▶ "Therefore," Paul says, since he is a minster of the new covenant with its life-giving energy, the style of his ministry must reflect this. In what ways does Paul conduct (or *not* conduct) his ministry to reflect the values of the new covenant (v. 2)?

▶ What do verses 4-6 tell us about Jesus?

▶ In verses 7-12 Paul explains that God has chosen imperfect humans to carry the glorious message of Christ. Why do you think God did this?

▶ Notice how being a vessel of such glorious news helps Paul maintain confidence and strength in the face of hardships. What does that say to you?

▶ What hope keeps Paul going (vv. 17-18)?

4. THIS WORLD IS NOT MY HOME (5:1-10)

An old gospel song says, "This world is not my home; I'm just a-passin' through." Paul's thoughts at the end of chapter 4 seem to launch him into a similar vein of thought.

Read verses 1-10 and then answer these questions:

▶ During his missionary journeys Paul frequently faced the very real possibility that he might die at any moment—from shipwreck, from wild beasts, or from angry mobs. How do you think these events in his life influenced the first verse of this chapter?

▶ Most people would probably say that they would prefer not to die. In fact, most of us do everything in our power to prolong life as long as possible. How does Paul's attitude in verses 2-4 differ?

▶ What gives Paul the confidence he talks about in verse 6?

▶ Do you consider verses 9-10 a threat or a promise? What makes the difference?

5. NEW CREATIONS (5:11—6:2)

Paul's life was spent taking the gospel to people who had never heard of Christ. What drove him to do this? Guilt? Fear? An attempt to appease God? In these verses he allows us to see into his heart for the answer.

Read these verses and then answer these questions:

▶ At first glance, it appears that Paul is serving God out of fear (v. 11). But is Paul referring to his fear of God, or the fear that people who do not know God will experience at the end of life? (Read verse 10 for a clue.)

▶ What does Christ's love compel Paul to do (v. 14)?

▶ Verse 17 is perhaps one of the greatest verses in the New Testament. Meditate for a few moments on this verse, and then write what it means to you.

▶ To "reconcile" means to bring two parties together who have been separated by disagreement. God and humankind have been separated by humanity's willfulness and selfishness. According to verses 18-19, who has taken the first step in achieving a reconciliation?

▶ As "Christ's ambassadors" (v. 20), what is our job?

▶ Verses 17-21 form another capsule gospel. If this were all of the Bible that existed, what would you know?

Discovery Group

STUDY SCRIPTURE: 2 Corinthians 3:7—6:2

KEY VERSE: 2 Corinthians 5:19

"Blest Be the Tie That Binds"

All of their friends were worried. Jesse and Luke had been best friends since sixth grade. And now they weren't speaking to each other.

It started last week when Luke borrowed Jesse's car for a date. Jesse had loaned Luke his car many times. (In fact, some people weren't even sure which boy actually *owned* the car, since both seemed to drive it equally as much.) But this time there was a problem.

After Luke's date he parked the car in front of Jesse's house and put the keys in the ashtray, as always. The next morning when Jesse went outside, he noticed a scratch all along the passenger's side. It looked like either someone had dragged a key or a knife along the car, or else the driver of the car had scraped it against something.

Jesse immediately called Luke to find out what had happened, but Luke denied knowing anything about the damage. Before Jesse could say anything else, Luke started yelling and saying that it was unfair for Jesse to blame him. Then he hung up.

The next day at school Luke avoided Jesse, even when they had the same class. By lunch everyone knew that something was wrong.

As the days went by, several of their friends tried to get Luke and Jesse back together. Luke was adamant that he would not apologize first. Jesse insisted that he had nothing to apologize for. Their friends knew that as soon as one of them took the first step, it would all be over. But neither boy would initiate the reconciliation.

God Takes the First Step

We know that because of humankind's failure to love and obey God—beginning in the Garden of Eden—an estrangement, or separation, occurred. God was on one side of the gulf, and all humanity was on the other side.

Paul gives us several verses in 2 Corinthians 4—6 that explain what happened next. Read these verses and then answer the questions that follow:

● "For God, who said, 'Let light shine out of darkness,' made his light shine in our hearts to give us the light of the knowledge of the glory of God in the face of Christ" (4:6).

● "And [Christ] died for all, that those who live should no longer live for themselves but for him who died for them and was raised again" (5:15).

- "Therefore, if anyone is in Christ, he is a new creation; the old has gone, the new has come!" (5:17).

- "All this is from God, who reconciled us to himself through Christ" (5:18).

- "God was reconciling the world to himself in Christ, not counting men's sins against them" (5:19).

- "God made him who had no sin to be sin for us, so that in him we might become the righteousness of God" (5:21).

- "In the time of my favor I heard you, and in the day of salvation I helped you" (6:2).

1. Who took the first step in reconciliation, God or humankind?

2. What step did God take to reconcile humanity to himself?

3. What punishment did God demand before humanity could be reconciled?

The Ministry of Reconciliation

Since God reconciled humanity to himself through Christ's atoning sacrifice, what does that mean for those of us who are Christians? Paul talks about that too:

- "Since, then, we know what it is to fear the Lord, we try to persuade men" (5:11).

- "For Christ's love compels us" (5:14).

- "All this is from God, who reconciled us to himself through Christ and gave us the ministry of reconciliation" (5:18).

- "And he has committed to us the message of reconciliation" (5:19).

- "We are therefore Christ's ambassadors, as though God were making his appeal through us" (5:20).

1. What does it mean to have "the ministry of reconciliation"?

2. What is the "message of reconciliation"?

3. How can we be "Christ's ambassadors"?

"Be Reconciled to God"

If you are not a Christian, God has taken the first step to reconcile you to himself: Christ died for your sins so that there would be no cause for separation. He invites you to be made "a new creation." How do you do that?

1. Recognize that God loves you and has offered you reconciliation.

2. Admit that there is a separation between you and God caused by ignorance and by willful disobedience.

3. Be genuinely sorry for the sin and rebellion in your heart.

4. Accept God's offer of reconciliation by inviting Christ into your life as Lord and Savior.

If you are already a Christian, consider seriously Paul's challenge to become a "minister of reconciliation." What can you do *this week* to respond to that challenge? How can you share the "message of reconciliation" with your friends?

10 Unequal Yokes

STUDY SCRIPTURE: 2 Corinthians 6:3—7:16

KEY VERSE: "Do not be yoked together with unbelievers" (2 Corinthians 6:14).

Personal Discovery

1. OVERVIEW

In these chapters Paul again returns to specific problems in the Corinthian church, especially their attacks on him.

Read 2 Corinthians 6:3—7:16 at one sitting, and then answer these questions:

▶ What do you think is the tone or mood of these chapters?

▶ Are there verses in these chapters that are difficult for you to understand?

▶ Are there verses in these chapters that seem to speak directly to you?

▶ What question would you like to ask about these chapters?

2. PAUL SPEAKS STERNLY TO HIS CHILDREN (6:3-13)

As we have noted before, there was apparently a large group in Corinth that had been attacking Paul. Frequently in both 1 and 2 Corinthians, Paul has reluctantly had to defend his honor and his ministry. These verses form one of the sternest of these defenses.

Read 6:3-13 and then answer these questions:

▶ If you are reading out of the *New International Version*, Paul says that he and the other apostles "commend" themselves (v. 4). An earlier version of the NIV says, "We show ourselves to be servants of God." Do you think Paul defends himself and his ministry so many times for his own benefit? Or is there another reason why the Corinthians need to have confidence in the apostle?

▶ In verses 4-5 Paul lists some of the hardships he has suffered. Read also 2 Corinthians 1:8-9 and 4:8-9. How would you describe the life of an apostle?

▶ In verses 6-7 Paul shifts from listing hardships to listing the way in which he responded to the hardships. Why is it so important for Paul to include these things in his listing?

▶ In verses 8-10 Paul lists nine contrasting states. Read through these slowly. How would you feel if you encountered these things?

▶ Finally, in verses 11-13 Paul speaks directly to the Corinthians who have attacked him. What does he ask of them? Do you think his request is fair?

3. WHAT GOES AROUND COMES AROUND (6:14—7:1)

These verses seem to form a kind of parenthesis in Paul's thinking, since 7:2 seems to connect so neatly to 6:13. Perhaps at some point during the early centuries these verses got out of place. Or perhaps an idea came to Paul as he was dictating this letter, and he wanted to discuss it while it was on his mind. Regardless, there are some very important instructions in this section.

After you have read these verses, answer these questions:

▶ Paul says quite strictly, "Do not be yoked together with unbelievers" (v. 14). This verse is often used to discourage young Christians from marrying non-Christians, and certainly that would be included in what Paul is saying. But he is also talking about other kinds of relationships. In what ways can a Christian unwisely become "yoked together" with non-Christians?

▶ Paul goes on in verses 14-16 to ask five questions that really all ask the same thing. He does this, of course, for emphasis. Obviously the apostle feels strongly about this point. What do these five questions really say? (Note: *Belial* is another name for Satan.)

▶ Remember that Corinth was a busy city with a lot of pagan idolatry, including many temples to many heathen gods. It was hard for the Corinthian Christians to avoid contact with all the idol worship. (Remember the discussion in 1 Corinthians 8:1-13 about eating meat that had been sacrificed to idols?) Why is Paul so concerned that the Christians will mingle too much with their heathen countrymen?

► In the Old Testament quotations in verses 17-18, it is clear that God expects Christians to avoid contact with non-Christians. Does that mean all contact? Are we to isolate ourselves completely from non-Christians? Read John 17:15-16 and 1 Corinthians 5:9-10. What light do these verses shed on this question?

► Obviously you cannot avoid contact with non-Christians. Indeed, you *should* not avoid that contact. Remember what Paul has just said about our being ministers of reconciliation and Christ's ambassadors (5:18-20)? How can we follow his instructions in the last chapter and the ones in this chapter at the same time? (Hint: What kind of relationships should we have with nonbelievers?)

► Think about the relationships you have with non-Christians. Do you think Paul (and God) would approve of them?

4. AGAIN PAUL SPEAKS TO HIS CHILDREN (7:2-7)

Paul now picks up the thought he left in 6:13. Review 6:3-13 before reading this passage. The apostle is still dealing with those who have attacked him.

After you have read these verses, answer these questions:

► In 6:13 Paul called the Corinthians "my children." How do verses 2-4 sound like a father speaking?

► Go back and read 2:12-13 before you read 7:5. Why was Paul so distressed before he heard from Titus?

► What news did Titus bring Paul (v. 7)?

5. SORROW BRINGS REPENTANCE (7:8-16)

Here Paul talks again about a previous letter (see 2:3-4). This might be a reference to 1 Corinthians or to another letter that has been lost. In either case, it must have been a stern letter, because it caused the Corinthians much sorrow.

Read these verses and then answer these questions:

▶ Paul says that he is not sorry, indeed he is happy, that his letter caused them so much sorrow. Why does he say this (v. 9)?

▶ Notice again that Paul talks about discipline being *redemptive* rather than *punitive* (or punishing). We've seen that before in 2:5-11. That's a very important distinction for us to make. What is the difference? How can discipline be redemptive rather than punitive?

▶ What is the difference between "godly sorrow" and "worldly sorrow" (v. 10)?

▶ What do verses 13-16 indicate about the relationship between Paul and the Corinthians? How is this different from 6:11-13?

Discovery Group

STUDY SCRIPTURE: 2 Corinthians 6:3—7:16

KEY VERSE: 2 Corinthians 6:14

The Odd Couple

Imagine this: One day you're flipping through channels on the old TV when you hear the announcer say, "On the next 'Donahue': Christians who got too close to non-Christians." *Wow,* you think, *I've got to see this!*

So the next day you tune in to "Donahue" to see what's happening. There are three people on the stage, and you listen as they tell their stories:

PEGGY: I was only 17 when I started dating Phil. My parents were against it from the beginning. See, we were a church family, pretty religious. But Phil's family never went to church. Phil wasn't what you would call wild, but he did like to have fun. After we graduated from high school we got married, over my parents' objections. At first, I continued going to church. Phil said he didn't mind, but I could always tell he wasn't too happy when I left. So I started cutting back on church attendance just to keep peace in the house. Pretty soon we were going camping on the weekends—or skiing, or boating. Even when we stayed home, we had lots to do. Before long, I wasn't attending church at all. That's when Phil started moving up in the company and being invited to all sorts of parties. Naturally I went with him. Phil never was a heavy drinker, but he did drink. It wasn't long before I did too. After a couple of years, I realized that I wasn't even praying anymore.

MARVIN: After I graduated from college, I went into business with my roommate. We were equal partners in a lumber supply business. Things were great the first few years. We were making really good money. Then the recession hit and things got tight. Ron, my partner, suggested some ways that we could save money. I was all for that, except that the ways he was suggesting weren't quite legal—things like keeping some of our profits hidden from the IRS, underpaying some of our younger employees, stuff like that. Because we were equal partners, we both had to agree on everything. It became very difficult to work with Ron. Finally, I sold my half of the business and got out. It just wasn't worth my spiritual health to keep the business.

TREVOR: Randy and I were best friends all through high school and college. We even both got married on the same day. We were each other's best man! Randy and his wife and my wife and I did everything together. Everything, that is, except go to church. Carol and I were Christians. Randy and Brenda weren't. When Randy joined a men's social club, he asked me to join too. I went with him once, but I didn't feel too comfortable. After all, everyone was drinking and gambling and just generally behaving atrociously. So I told him I wouldn't join. But he kept at me, and eventually I gave in. The club also had a lot of weekend activities, especially on Sunday. In order to keep my membership, I had to attend a certain number of these activities. Eventually missing that much church and being around those guys really hurt my spiritual life. I know Randy wouldn't purposely hurt me for anything, but he just doesn't understand spiritual things.

Yoked with Unbelievers

In Deuteronomy 22:10 it says, "Do not plow with an ox and a donkey yoked together." That's a very practical piece of advice, because oxen and donkeys are very different-sized beasts. That's like trying to make a seesaw work with a two-year-old kid and a linebacker for the Steelers. But what does plowing have to do with us?

1. In 2 Corinthians 6:14 Paul says, "Do not be yoked together with unbelievers." Then he goes on to ask five questions. Answer each of his questions in the spaces below:

  a. "What do righteousness and wickedness have in common?"

  b. "What fellowship can light have with darkness?"

  c. "What harmony is there between Christ and Belial [Satan]?"

d. "What does a believer have in common with an unbeliever?"

  e. "What agreement is there between the temple of God and idols?"

  2. In 6:17-18 Paul cites two quotations from the Old Testament. Read these quotations and then put them into your own words:

In the World but Not of It

So what are we supposed to do—lock ourselves up in monasteries and convents, withdraw from school and start our own, or move off into the country so that we don't have to associate with non-Christians? Over the centuries many have tried to do these things. (Some people still advocate this kind of action.) Maybe someday we can colonize a planet just for Christians!

Read John 17:15-16 and 1 Corinthians 5:9-10. These verses seem to indicate that we *have* to associate with nonbelievers (nothing else makes sense!). Read also 2 Corinthians 5:18-20. These verses indicate that we are to be "Christ's ambassadors" to unbelievers. We *have* to associate with them in order to share the gospel with them. The question, then, is this:

What kind of associations with nonbelievers are OK, and what kind of associations are not OK?

What do you think?

Association Analysis

1. In the first column below list 10 people you believe are non-Christians with whom you associate on a daily or weekly basis. In the second column find a one- or two-word description for the relationship you have with each person ("best friend," "boyfriend," "lab partner," etc.). Then in

the third column indicate how close you feel to each person by writing a number from 1 to 5, with 1 being "not very close" and 5 being "very close."

Person's Name	Type of Association	How Close
a.		
b.		
c.		
d.		
e.		
f.		
g.		
h.		
i.		
j.		

2. Now look back at your list. Concentrate especially on anyone whose relationship you have evaluated with a closeness rating of 4 or 5. Ask yourself these questions:

    a. Do you think these individuals exert much influence over you?

    b. How much? Is it too much?

c. Do any of these relationships jeopardize your spiritual condition or growth?

d. Have any of these individuals ever pressured you to do something you felt would be wrong for a Christian to do?

e. Do these individuals respect your beliefs and values?

f. What do you need to do to keep these relationships from hurting your spiritual life?

11 The Gift That Keeps On Giving

STUDY SCRIPTURE: 2 Corinthians 8:1—9:15

KEY VERSE: "Each man should give what he has decided in his heart to give, not reluctantly or under compulsion, for God loves a cheerful giver" (2 Corinthians 9:7).

Personal Discovery

1. OVERVIEW

In these two chapters Paul returns to a topic he wrote about in his first letter: the offering (see 1 Corinthians 16:1-3). Most of the members of the Early Church were in the lower economic strata of society. It was necessary for the Christians to collect offerings to help each other out. (Some things never change!) At first glance, these chapters seem to be just about ancient lands and ancient problems. But there is much here that applies to us too.

Read chapters 8 and 9, then answer these questions:

▶ Is there any verse in these chapters that particularly catches your attention?

▶ Is there a verse that confuses or bothers you?

▶ Does it irritate or bore you to read about money? What do you *feel* as you read these chapters?

▶ If you could summarize these two chapters in one sentence, what would that be?

▶ How open are you for the Holy Spirit to speak to you as you study these chapters?

2. GIVE GENEROUSLY (8:1-15)

We discover by reading Romans 15:26 and 1 Corinthians 16:1-4 that Paul was collecting money for the church in Jerusalem, the headquarters of Christianity. The believers there were quite impoverished. As we read these verses, and the ones that follow, we can find principles and guidelines for us today.

Read 8:1-15 and then answer these questions:

▶ The Christians in Macedonia were suffering intense persecution for their faith. Many of them had lost property, jobs, and material goods. And yet, according to Paul, what was their response to the offering?

▶ In verse 8 Paul says, "I am not commanding you." Why didn't he just order them to give?

▶ What is the supreme example for us in the matter of self-sacrifice and giving (v. 9)?

▶ Apparently Paul had been collecting this offering for a year (v. 10). What are the two principles for giving that we are shown in verse 12?

3. RESPONSIBLE MANAGEMENT OF THE OFFERING (8:16-24)

In this section Paul tells the Corinthians how the offering is being handled so that there will be no reason for suspicion or doubt.

Read these verses and then answer these questions:

▶ Knowing some of the criticism that Paul has endured from the Corinthians, why is it wise for the offering to be accompanied by several persons?

▶ Why is it still necessary today for church money to be handled in the safest and most responsible manner?

▶ Notice words like "enthusiasm" (v. 17), "eagerness" (v. 19), "liberal" (v. 20), and "zealous" (v. 22). What do these words tell us about the people involved in this offering, both the givers and the collectors?

▶ How do you feel about being asked to give money to the church?

4. CAREFUL PLANNING (9:1-5)

In this section the apostle gives the Corinthians some practical advice about planning for the collection.

Read these verses and then answer these questions:

▶ It is apparent that the Corinthians have known about this offering for a year (v. 2). Why do you think Paul cautions them to be ready (v. 3)?

▶ Look back at 1 Corinthians 16:2. What is the plan Paul gave them then in order to be ready?

▶ Why do you think we take an offering in our churches every week rather than just once a month or even once a year?

▶ What could be the result if the Corinthians aren't prepared for the offering and feel pressured at the last minute (v. 5)?

5. SOWING AND REAPING (9:6-15)

Paul has already stated principles about giving that apply to us as much as they did to the Corinthians. Now he is writing one of the best passages in the New Testament about Christian giving.

Read these verses and then answer these questions:

▶ Do you think Paul is setting up a mathematical formula in verse 6, something like *If you give $10.00, you'll receive $20.00 back?* Why not?

▶ In verse 7 Paul says how gifts should be given and how they should *not* be given. What are the "should" and "should nots"?

▶ Paul has already noted that the believers in Jerusalem, the recipients of the offering, are poverty-stricken and that the believers in Macedonia are also poor. How then can he say what he does in verses 8-11? Could he be talking about something other than money? If so, what?

▶ Have you ever received a blessing from being generous?

▶ What is the result of a generous offering for both the recipients and the givers (vv. 13-14)?

▶ When Paul says, "Thanks be to God for his indescribable gift!" (v. 15), he's not talking about the offering. What is he talking about?

Discovery Group

STUDY SCRIPTURE: 2 Corinthians 8:1—9:15

KEY VERSE: 2 Corinthians 9:7

Where Does All Your Money Go?

1. Think back over the last four or five weeks. How much money *out of your own pocket* do you usually spend in a month for the following items?

a. _____ Meals and snacks

b. _____ Clothes

c. _____ Records, cassettes, and CDs

d. _____ Recreation

e. _____ School supplies

f. _____ Cosmetics or other beauty/hygiene supplies

g. _____ Magazines, books, comic books

h. _____ Athletic equipment

i. _____ Transportation (gasoline, bus passes, etc.)

j. _____ Church offerings

2. How do you feel about giving money to the church? Check one (or more) of the following responses:

a. _____ I enjoy giving money to the church and do so cheerfully.

b. _____ I understand the need for offerings and give out of a sense of responsibility.

c. _____ I give because I know God wants me to and I want to please Him.

d. _____ I give because everyone expects me to.

e. _____ I give because my parents make me.

f. _____ I hate giving money to the church.

g. _____ I don't give money to the church.

Oh No, Not Another Offering!

In 2 Corinthians 8—9 Paul writes about an offering he is collecting for the Christians in Jerusalem. Let's suppose some of the Corinthians were really good at dodging offerings. Below are listed some of their responses. Find verses in these two chapters that answer their excuses and complaints.

v. ___ 1. "I really can't afford to give. I have enough trouble paying my bills."

v. ___ 2. "I have other gifts to share with the church. After all, I sing in the choir and teach a Sunday School class."

v. ___ 3. "I don't see anyone else giving."

v. ___ 4. "I can't give as much as others can."

v. ___ 5. "I just never seem to be ready for the offering plate when it comes by."

v. ___ 6. "I don't know why I should give. I never get anything back."

v. ___ 7. "Well, I give when someone talks me into it."

v. ___ 8. "I give, but I'm not happy about it."

v. ___ 9. "I don't think the people who benefit from the offering are grateful."

Where Does All the Church's Money Go?

How is the money collected in your church spent? Find out and write in the spaces below how much is spent (what percentage) and for what.

1. *Local Expenses*
   Salaries (pastor and others)...$ _____
   Building (mortgage, utilities, etc.) ....$ _____
   Sunday School materials ....$ _____
   Other program expenses ....$ _____

2. *District or Regional Expenses*
   District salaries ....$ _____
   District youth program ....$ _____
   Other district programs ....$ _____
   College support ....$ _____

3. *National or Global Expenses*
   National salaries ....$ _____
   Missionary salaries..$ _____
   Missions programs...$ _____
   Domestic social programs ....$ _____

A Model for Giving

"For you know the grace of our Lord Jesus Christ, that though he was rich, yet for your sakes he became poor, so that you through his poverty might become rich."   —2 Corinthians 8:9

"Thanks be to God for his indescribable gift!"   —2 Corinthians 9:15

12 Nobody Knows the Trouble I've Seen

STUDY SCRIPTURE: 2 Corinthians 10:1—11:33

KEY VERSE: "But this happened that we might not rely on ourselves but on God" (2 Corinthians 1:9).

Personal Discovery

1. OVERVIEW

As Paul is getting close to the end of the letter, he once again returns to the problem of the group in Corinth that is severely criticizing him. As we read, we must remember that these were the first decades of the Church. (This letter was probably written around A.D. 56-57.) There was little structure, no written policies or theology, no reference books (the four Gospels had not even been written yet). Keeping the gospel message pure and unchanged was a challenge. Doctrinal authority rested completely in the hands of the apostles.

So it wasn't just a personal problem to Paul that he was being attacked. It was a matter crucial to the survival of the Corinthian congregation as an authentic Christian church.

Read through chapters 10 and 11 at one sitting, and then answer these questions:

▶ Can you describe in one or two words what you think is the tone or mood of these chapters?

▶ What question or questions are you eager to have answered as we study this material?

► Is there a section in these chapters that particularly appeals to you?

► Is there anything in these chapters that bothers or concerns you?

2. APOSTOLIC TACTICS (10:1-6)

If you read this section, and the ones that follow, without an understanding of what must have been going on in Corinth, it could appear that Paul is a whiner and a braggart. But if we "read between the lines," we can discover the kind of attacks against which Paul is defending himself.

Read these verses and then answer these questions:

► We can identify one of the attacks by reading verse 1 along with verse 10 from the next section. What seems to be the complaint that some have lodged against the apostle?

► Verse 2 gives us a clue to another accusation. What is it? What do you think living "by the standards of this world" could mean?

► Verses 4-6 sound very strong and assertive. What do you think brought Paul to speaking this way?

3. THE LIMITS OF BOASTING (10:7-18)

In this section we continue to get a "profile" of the individuals in Corinth who have been attacking Paul. And we begin to realize that these individuals are not all just members of the Corinthian congregation. There seem to be people who have come to Corinth from elsewhere and who have tried to take on an authoritative role in the church at Corinth. They have been trying to establish their authority by undermining Paul's.

Read these verses, and then answer these questions:

▶ What do you think was the attack that prompted Paul to write verse 7?

▶ In verse 10 we hit again the same complaints we found in verse 1. Remember that when Paul was first at Corinth, he was teaching the gospel and winning new converts. Refer back to what Paul said in 1 Corinthians 9:19-23 about his tactics for winning converts. What about his work might have made him appear to be "timid" (v. 1) or "unimpressive" (v. 10)?

▶ In the time since Paul was first in Corinth, many problems have plagued the congregation, some caused by insiders and some by outsiders. Why might that cause Paul to adapt a different tone ("bold," v. 1; "weighty and forceful," v. 10) in his letters?

▶ In reading verse 12, what picture do you get of the people Paul is writing about?

▶ From what Paul is saying in verses 13-16, we can construct a scenario that includes these other "authorities" moving into Corinth and taking credit for Paul's work there. How does Paul respond to their actions?

▶ Verse 18 gives us a little philosophy that we should all remember. Do you know people who boast about their spirituality or their good deeds? What does this verse say to such a person?

4. "SUPER-APOSTLES" (11:1-15)

In this section Paul gets a little more specific about the people he has been responding to. We don't have to read between the lines as much to identify their actions.

Read these verses and then answer these questions:

▶ We must constantly remember that Paul pioneered the evangelization of Corinth. That makes him the spiritual father of this congregation. What kind of fatherly hopes and fears does he reveal in verses 2-3?

▶ In verse 5, Paul calls his opponents "super-apostles." Obviously that is a bit of irony or sarcasm. But it does give us a clue about how these individuals were apparently behaving and what they were claiming. What does verse 4 tell us about the message these "super-apostles" were preaching?

▶ In verse 6 we get the idea that maybe these other leaders were trained orators, and they had been laughing at Paul because he wasn't. If we watch Sunday TV, we can see many gifted speakers who are smooth and impressive. They are better "performers" than most of the pastors who fill pulpits in local congregations each Sunday. Does that mean that the TV preachers are more knowledgeable or more authentic than your preacher?

▶ In 1 Corinthians 9, Paul defended the right of an apostle to be supported by the church in which he is ministering. And yet, both in that passage and in this one, he indicates that he did *not* allow the Corinthians to contribute to his support while he was there. Somehow the "super-apostles" were using that fact against Paul (vv. 7-9). How do you think they managed to do this?

▶ It is very obvious that this self-defense, which Paul calls "boasting," is uncomfortable for the apostle. So why does he do it (v. 12)?

▶ In verses 13-15 Paul takes off the gloves and identifies his opponents for what they really are: "deceitful workmen" and servants of Satan. Does this help you understand why Paul is so concerned about their influence in Corinth?

5. APOSTLES SHOULD GET HAZARDOUS DUTY PAY! (11:16-33)

In this section Paul continues his "boasting." Remember that this is not just a matter of personal pride to Paul. It is a matter that affects the very destiny of the Corinthian church.

Read these verses and then answer these questions:

▶ In verses 18-20 Paul paints a pretty unflattering picture of the false apostles who were trying to take over the Corinthian church. How did these individuals treat the Corinthian believers?

▶ In verse 22 we get another clue to the identity of these false apostles. They were apparently Jews who were using their Hebrew heritage to make them appear more authoritative. Perhaps the greatest controversy in the first-century Church, one that threatened to split and even destroy the Church, was whether pagans converted to Christianity had to convert to Judaism also.

Read Acts 15:1-35. How does the seriousness of this controversy illuminate Paul's concern in these chapters?

▶ Beginning in verse 23, Paul resorts to a list of the hardships and atrocities he has endured in carrying out his ministry as an apostle. Read through this list slowly, allowing your mind to create an image of each of the things Paul mentions. Remember that Paul isn't doing this to get sympathy. He is defending his position as the genuine authority over the church at Corinth. How does this list of adversities support his claim?

▶ Go back and read 2 Corinthians 1:3-11; 4:7-12; and 6:4-10. How do these previous passages differ from the one in chapter 11?

Discovery Group

STUDY SCRIPTURE: 2 Corinthians 10:1—11:33
KEY VERSE: 2 Corinthians 1:9

A Catalog of Calamities

1. Listed below are some of the things that teenagers have to face. Rank these in order from 1 to 12, with 1 being the easiest to handle and 12 being the toughest:

a. ___ Finding out your parents are getting a divorce

b. ___ Failing a test you studied for

c. ___ Losing your lunch money

d. ___ Breaking up with your girlfriend/boyfriend

e. ___ Failing to be elected as cheerleader, team captain, student body president, or other desired honor

f. ___ Having your best friend move out of town

g. ___ Having one of your friends die

h. ___ Being laughed at for being a Christian

i. ___ Falling down the stairs at school

j. ___ Moving to a new city

k. ___ Being rejected for a date

l. ___ Discovering you have to get braces on your teeth

Now answer these questions:

2. What is the worst thing that has happened to you in the last week?

3. What is the worst thing that has happened to you in the last month?

4. What is the worst thing that has happened to you in the last year?

5. What is the worst thing that has happened to you in your entire life?

You'll Never Believe
What Happened to Me

Imagine for a few moments that you are an insurance underwriter, responsible for evaluating the potential risk involved in insuring a person and designing an insurance policy that will protect the individual without bankrupting the company.

The apostle Paul has come to your company to apply for travel insurance. As part of the form you have asked him to complete, he is supposed to give you a description of the types of dangers and hardships he has faced during his past travels.

1. Read the passages below and make a list of what Paul would have to put on his insurance application:

    a. 2 Corinthians 4:8-9

    b. 2 Corinthians 6:4-10

    c. 2 Corinthians 11:23-28, 32-33

2. Now examine how Paul feels about these trials and tribulations. From the passages below, find clues about Paul's attitudes and reactions to all this trouble:

    a. 2 Corinthians 1:3-11

b. 2 Corinthians 4:8-9, 16-18

c. 2 Corinthians 6:4-10

A Teen in Trouble

Imagine that you have a good Christian friend named Sean living in another city. One day in the mail you get this letter from him:

Dear friend,

This has been the worst week of my life. You remember in my last letter how I told you I thought there was something funny going on between my mom and my dad? I really thought they were getting a divorce or something. Well, it's not that bad—but almost.

Last Sunday night my dad called a "family meeting." We all knew there was something big, because he never does that. Well, he announced that his company is sending him to Saudi Arabia for a year. *A whole year!* I couldn't believe my ears. Then he made an even more devastating announcement. Mom, my two sisters, and I are going to live with my grandparents in Ohio while Dad is gone. They live in this dinky little town in the middle of nowhere. It's a great place to visit, but who wants to *live* there? And it will be my senior year! Instead of graduating here, where all my friends are, I'll be graduating from Podunk High. Imagine what that will look like to all the colleges I plan on applying to.

As soon as our little meeting was over, I called my girlfriend and gave her the news. She burst into tears, right on the phone. I felt like a complete heel.

You know I had a good chance of getting the lead in next year's musical, and I was planning on starting for the football team. But now that's all washed up. And the church in my grandparents' town is really bad news. There are like two teenagers there, and they're both dweebs.

I hate to say it, but I kinda wish it had been a divorce. At least we would be staying in the same town.

I am totally bummed out about this. I begged my parents to let me stay here. I could live with Kevin, my friend from next door. But they said absolutely not. I have to go with my mom to be the "man of the family." That's total garbage.

I am so mad at my dad for accepting the assignment. He says he doesn't have any choice, but I know he could turn it down if he really wanted to. He is absolutely ruining my life. I've thought about running away. I've even thought about killing myself. Dying would be better than living with my grandparents for a year.

I don't know what to do. I guess there isn't anything I *can* do. I don't suppose you've got any ideas?

How would you respond to Sean? Write him a letter here:

Perplexed, but Not in Despair

Look back at the first activity and the things you wrote there that have happened to you. Choose the one thing that is giving you the most trouble. (Or, if some other problem has occurred to you, use it.)

Based on what you have learned in this lesson, what can you do to make the problem more endurable and to keep it from ruining your spiritual life?

13 Turning Disabilities into Abilities

STUDY SCRIPTURE: 2 Corinthians 12:1—13:14

KEY VERSE: "But he said to me, 'My grace is sufficient for you, for my power is made perfect in weakness.' Therefore I will boast all the more gladly about my weaknesses, so that Christ's power may rest on me" (2 Corinthians 12:9).

Personal Discovery

1. OVERVIEW

We are now approaching the end of our study. In these last two chapters Paul wraps up his self-defense, gives the Corinthians some final warnings, and assures them of his love.

Read these chapters at one sitting, and then answer these questions:

▷ Is there anything in these chapters that makes you uncomfortable or irritated?

▷ Is there anything in these chapters that makes you happy?

▷ What section of these chapters do you think you need help understanding?

▷ What question would you like to have answered about these chapters?

2. WEAK AND STRONG (12:1-10)

Paul is continuing his "boasting"—his defense in the face of criticism. As he does so, he reveals some intimate details of his life. These details show us one of the highest points and one of the lowest points of the apostle's spiritual journey.

Read these verses and then answer these questions:

▶ Paul finished chapter 11 by "boasting" about the hardships and disasters he has faced. Now he is going to go the other extreme and tell about one of the high points of his life. It is pretty clear that the apostle is talking about himself when he says, "I know a man in Christ" (v. 2). Why do you think Paul feels it necessary to tell the story in verses 2-5 as if it had happened to someone else?

▶ Why do you think Paul gives so few details about what happened when he had his vision?

▶ In verse 7 Paul says that he has been given a "thorn" in his flesh. Over the centuries many have speculated about what this thorn might be. Nearly every medical condition or deformity has been suggested. Why do you think Paul does not reveal what it is?

▶ Notice in verse 8 that Paul prayed three times to have this "thorn" removed. But the Lord did not heal him. If such a great Christian as Paul does not get what he prays for, what does that say about prayer?

▶ Even though God didn't answer Paul's prayer in the way Paul wanted Him to, He did answer. What was God's response to Paul's request (v. 9)?

▶ What was the eventual result of Paul having to continue to suffer with his "thorn" (v. 9)?

▶ What does Paul mean when he says, "When I am weak, then I am strong" (v. 10)?

3. THE APOSTLE IS COMING TO TOWN (12:11-21)

As Paul is wrapping up his self-defense, he gives the Corinthians notice that he is planning a third visit with them. He is not sure, however, that the visit will be pleasant for anyone involved.

Read these verses and then answer these questions:

▶ How have the Corinthians driven Paul to make a "fool" of himself (v. 11)?

▶ How does Paul write like a father in verses 14-15?

▶ What are Paul's fears about his upcoming visit to Corinth (vv. 20-21)?

4. THIS IS YOUR LAST WARNING (13:1-14)

At the end of this long and difficult letter, Paul concludes with some final warnings for the Corinthians.

Read this chapter and then answer these questions:

▶ What does Paul mean when he says that Christ "was crucified in weakness" (v. 4)?

▶ How is Paul's "weakness" similar to that of Christ?

▶ Paul instructs the Corinthians to examine themselves (v. 5). What is it they are examining themselves for?

▶ Paul has spoken quite harshly to the Corinthians in this letter. What reason does he give for his harshness (v. 10)?

5. GOOD-BYE, 2 CORINTHIANS

Congratulations! You have now finished one of the most difficult books in the New Testament. Before we leave it finally, however, let's take a few minutes to review. Look back over the 13 chapters. If your Bible version has section headings, read those and a couple of verses in each section. Read again any verse you may have marked during our study. Then flip back through the pages of this study book, and reread your responses to the questions.

After you have done that, spend a few moments answering these questions:

▶ What section of this letter gave you the most trouble? Why?

▶ If you had a few moments with the apostle Paul right now, what would you say to him?

▶ What would you say to a friend that was considering a study of 2 Corinthians?

▶ What is the most important thing you learned from this study?

▶ How do you think this study will change your life?

Discovery Group

STUDY SCRIPTURE: 2 Corinthians 12:1—13:14

KEY VERSE: 2 Corinthians 12:9

Personal Inventory

Check any of the following attributes that you think describe you:

☐ beautiful	☐ stupid	☐ athletic
☐ clumsy	☐ attractive	☐ shy
☐ fat	☐ awkward	☐ confused
☐ dumb	☐ confident	☐ fearful
☐ talented	☐ uncreative	☐ slow
☐ uncoordinated	☐ weak	☐ caring
☐ personable	☐ skinny	☐ short
☐ ugly	☐ smart	☐ moody
☐ outgoing	☐ fearless	☐ depressed
☐ unstable	☐ popular	☐ strong
☐ bright	☐ creative	☐ mature
☐ gifted	☐ plain	☐ self-confident
☐ friendly	☐ sickly	☐ loving
☐ unpopular	☐ insightful	☐ timid

1. What do you think is your greatest strength?

2. What do you think is your greatest weakness?

A Thorn in the Flesh

Pretend that you are writing a magazine article about successful people who have overcome disabilities. Someone has suggested that you research the life of the apostle Paul. Look at 2 Corinthians 12:7-10 and answer these questions:

1. What type of disability did Paul have?

2. How serious was this disability?

3. Did God remove Paul's disability when he prayed for healing?

4. How *did* God answer Paul's prayer?

5. How did Paul's attitude about his disability change?

6. What did Paul learn to substitute for his disability?

7. What does "When I am weak, then I am strong" (v. 10) mean?

8. What became of Paul's life?

Turning Weaknesses to Strengths

Jim Abbot pitched for the U.S. Olympic team and later became a pitcher for the California Angels, despite the fact that he was born with only one hand.

Beethoven became deaf halfway through his career and still composed some of his greatest works, including his Fifth and Ninth symphonies.

Nelson Rockefeller overcame dyslexia to become a successful businessman and vice president of the United States.

Stephen Hawking, one of the greatest theoretical physicists of our age (some consider him to be the most brilliant man in physics since Albert Einstein), has amyotrophic lateral sclerosis (Lou Gehrig's disease); yet he continues to write, teach, and make guest appearances even though he cannot walk, stand, or feed himself. Neither can he speak. He communicates through a computerized voice synthesizer that he controls with the fingers of his left hand (he has lost the use of his right hand).

Thomas Edison, the inventor of the light bulb and the phonograph, was partially deaf and suffered from dyslexia.

Helen Keller, although deaf and blind from childhood, became a world-famous author, speaker, and advocate of rights for the disabled.

Fanny Crosby became blind during infancy due to an infection and the malpractice of a country doctor, yet went on to write several thousand hymns, including "Rescue the Perishing," "Pass Me Not, O Gentle Savior," "All the Way My Saviour Leads Me," and "Praise Him! Praise Him!" She once said, "Years ago I made up my mind to make the best of everything. In my quiet moments I say to myself, 'Fanny, there are many worse things than blindness that might have happened to you. On the whole it has been a good thing that I *have* been blind. How in the world could I have lived such a helpful life as I have lived had I not been blind? I am very well satisfied. I never let anything trouble me, and to my implicit faith, and to my implicit trust in my Heavenly Father's goodness, I attribute my good health and long life."

Joni Eareckson Tada suffered a spinal cord injury in a diving accident while still a teenager, leaving her paralyzed from the neck down. Nonetheless, she learned to paint by holding a brush in her teeth. She went on to be an internationally known writer and speaker. She has traveled extensively, speaking from her wheelchair of her faith in God.

"When I Am Weak, Then I Am Strong"

All of us have disabilities, weaknesses, characteristics that threaten to handicap us. But those negative things don't need to destroy us or rob us of a full and effective life.

Look back at what you listed in the first activity as your greatest weakness. What can you do to turn this into a strength?

"I will boast all the more gladly about my weaknesses, so that Christ's power may rest on me."   —2 Corinthians 12:9